THE **MINI** ROUGH GUIDE TO
GUERNSEY

ROUGH
GUIDES

YOUR TAILOR-MADE TRIP STARTS HERE

Tailor-made trips and unique adventures crafted by local experts

Rough Guides has been inspiring travellers for more than 35 years. Leave it to our local experts to create your perfect itinerary and book it at local rates.

Don't follow the crowd – find your own path.

HOW ROUGHGUIDES.COM/TRIPS WORKS

STEP 1 Pick your dream destination, tell us what you want and submit an enquiry.

STEP 2 Fill in a short form to tell your local expert about your dream trip and preferences.

STEP 3 Our local expert will craft your tailor-made itinerary. You'll be able to tweak and refine it until you're completely satisfied.

STEP 4 Book online with ease, pack your bags and enjoy the trip! Our local expert will be on hand 24/7 while you're on the road.

PLAN AND BOOK YOUR TRIP AT ROUGHGUIDES.COM/TRIPS

HOW TO DOWNLOAD YOUR FREE EBOOK

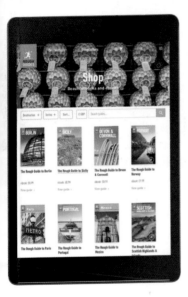

1. Visit **www.roughguides.com/free-ebook** or scan the **QR code** below

2. Enter the code **guernsey670**

3. Follow the simple step-by-step instructions

For troubleshooting contact: mail@roughguides.com

10 THINGS NOT TO MISS

A PERFECT DAY

9.00am

Breakfast. Christies in the heart of St Peter Port (41 Le Pollet, open from 9am, closed Sun) offers a coffee-and-croissant fix or a full English breakfast. Watch the world go by or secure a seat on the balcony for lovely harbour views.

10.00am

Picture-postcard port. Explore the cobbled streets of St Peter Port, stroll along the waterfront to Cornet Castle or up to Hauteville House, where Victor Hugo penned *Les Misérables*.

Noon

Cliff walk. For views that inspired Impressionist painter, Renoir, take the first section of the south coast cliff path starting at South Esplanade in St Peter Port and ending at Fermain Bay, one of Guernsey's prettiest beaches. (Allow at least an hour as there are quite a few steps).

1.00pm

Lunch break. Fermain Beach Café has the best fresh crab sandwiches on the island and a lovely terrace on the beach. Alternatively, splash out and lunch at La Frégate (www.lafregatehotel.com) in St Peter Port, for Guernsey's best seafood and a terrace with a sublime view out to Herm and Sark — even as far as the coast of France on a clear day.

3.00pm

West Coast. Head west to Rocquaine Bay where Fort Grey's Shipwreck Museum tells the grim story of vessels wrecked

IN **GUERNSEY**

on the rock-strewn coasts. Portelet Harbour southwest of Fort Grey has a pretty sandy cove, ideal for a dip if the tide is out.

5.00pm

Vazon Bay. Further along the coast watch or join the surfers on the golden sands of Vazon Bay. Guernsey Surf School (www.guernseysurfschool.co.uk) hires out all the gear. Vistas Beach Café, right on the beach with a roof terrace, has great views.

6.00pm

Sunset cocktail. Continue along the coast to Cobo Bay and catch the last of the sun's rays on the spacious terrace of the Cobo Bay Hotel, a favourite spot for admiring the views.

8.00pm

Dining options. Return to St Peter Port for the best choice of restaurants. Indulge in a slap-up seafood dinner at Le Nautique (see page 107), Mora (see page 107) or Pier 17 (see page 108), all with harbour views. Ask for a seat by the window and watch the sunset over the marina.

10.00pm

On the town. RED, on the waterfront, has a cool cocktail bar (along with top-quality steaks); or for something more traditional try the Old Government House Hotel's Crown Club with its red leather seats and antique brass. Familiarly known as the OGH, and located up the hill from the main shopping street, this was the former residence of the governor of Guernsey.

CONTENTS

A NOTE TO READERS

At Rough Guides, we always strive to bring you the most up-to-date information. This book was produced during a period of continuing uncertainty caused by the Covid-19 pandemic, so please note that content is more subject to change than usual. We recommend checking the latest restrictions and official guidance.

OVERVIEW

Sitting just off the Cherbourg peninsula, it is not surprising that Guernsey and its little sister islands have a heady mix of French and British cultures. Author Victor Hugo, exiled to Jersey and then to Guernsey, where he wrote *Les Misérables*, felt perfectly at home in the Channel Islands, describing them as 'morsels of France fallen into the sea and gathered by England'. It was this fusion of French and English culture, along with superb scenery and the sunniest location in the British Isles, that appealed to UK visitors in the early days of tourism. Although not truly British, the Channel Islands have been linked with the British Crown for over 900 years, the official language is English, cash machines dispense sterling and you drive on the left.

Guernsey may be the most densely populated of the Channel Islands but it retains quaint rural lanes, fine sandy beaches and miles of spectacular cliffs in the south. The island has one of the largest tidal movements in the world, with waters retreating twice a day to reveal large expanses of golden sands and lunar-like seascapes, pierced with rocks and reefs. Along with traditional beach pursuits such as swimming, windsurfing and rock-pooling, there has been a growth in adrenalin-fuelled activities such as sunset abseiling, cliff face rock-climbing or coasteering explorations.

In the unlikely event you tire of the coast, Guernsey has monuments ranging from eerie Neolithic tombs to

Toads and Donkeys

Guernsey and Jersey run their affairs separately and there has been rivalry ever since they took opposing sides in the English Civil War. To this day, Jerseymen call Guernseymen *ânes* or donkeys while Guernseymen call Jerseymen *crapauds* or toads, there being no toads on Guernsey.

Sark's rocky coastline

Napoleonic towers and World War II bunkers and tunnels – potent reminders that the Channel Islands were the only the parts of the British Isles occupied by German forces. The south of the island offers 28 miles (45km) of cliff-top walks; and the network of Green Lanes, where traffic is restricted to 15mph (24kmh), was developed with walkers and cyclists in mind. Even on main roads the pace is slow, with a maximum speed limit of 35mph (56kmh). Not that the sedate speed limits deter the island's affluent residents from driving around in their plush Porsches. Walking and cycling may be encouraged but Guernsey has one of the highest rates of private vehicle ownership in the world. If you are hiring a car be prepared for traffic congestion, very narrow lanes and a quaint but frustrating absence of signposting.

LOCATION AND CLIMATE

Guernsey lies in the Gulf of St Malo, 31 miles (50km) west of the Normandy coast and 75 miles (120km) south of Weymouth. As a bailiwick it also embraces the smaller islands of Herm, Jethou, Sark and Alderney. Herm and Sark can be easily reached by ferry (20 and 50 minutes respectively) while Alderney, the most northerly of the Channel Islands, just eight miles (13km) from France, is more remote, taking 85 minutes by boat. In the summer the islands have a daily average of eight hours of sunshine and an average maximum temperature of 68°F (20°C). The best months to visit are from May to September, July and August being the hottest. Sea temperatures are chilly or refreshing, depending on how hardy you are, averaging 62.8°F (17.1°C) in summer.

'PECULIAR OF THE CROWN'

The Channel Islands have a quirky history and some unique, quasi-feudal customs. Termed a 'Peculiar of the Crown' they pledge allegiance directly to the English Crown, not to the parliament of the UK. As the last remaining territories of the dukes of Normandy, they toast the Queen of England as 'Our Duke of Normandy'. They

FRENCH SPICE

On a clear day you can see the French coast from Guernsey's Jerbourg Point. Geographically the Channel Islands belong naturally to France rather than to England and have a discernible Gallic veneer. The great French Impressionist, Pierre-Auguste Renoir, who appraised Guernsey's light with a painter's eye at Moulin Huet Bay, noticed how 'the Anglo-Saxon miss sheds her prudery when she arrives in Guernsey'. Victor Hugo, for his part, was prepared to broaden her mind still further: ignoring Anglo-Saxon decencies altogether, he lived on the island with both wife and mistress, introducing them respectively as *'Madame, la mère de mes enfants'* and *'Madame, mon amie'.*

are not full members of the EU, although when Britain joined in 1973, they were granted special privileges (this remains unchanged even though Britain left). The islands delegate matters of foreign policy and defence to the UK parliament but in other affairs they guard their independence zealously. Guernsey has its own government and legal system; it prints its own currency (including a £1 note) and issues its

Alderney post box and telephone kiosk

own stamps. Sark's constitution dates back to 1563 and its feudal form of government prevailed up until 2008 when, after months of infighting, the island held its first general election and Sark became Europe's newest democracy.

LANGUAGE

Guernésiais (also known as patois, Dgernésiais and Guernsey French) is the local dialect, derived from ancient Norman French. It was once the island's native tongue but has now all but disappeared as a language spoken in the home.

Large numbers of English settlers arrived on Guernsey in the 19th century, many of them officers retired on half pay, and by the end of the century English was the prevalent language of St Peter Port. The use of the dialect as the island's first language came to an end in the post-war period when the many children who had been evacuated during the German Occupation returned to the island speaking English. In all the country parishes, however, Guernésiais could still be heard spoken until the late 1960s. The written language can still be seen today in street names and surnames, and the Guernsey Tourist Information Office welcomes you with *'Bian v'nue a tous'*. A small number of over 65s speak Guernésiais but as a visitor you are unlikely to hear it apart from the occasional greeting between. Sercquiais, Sark's equivalent to Guernésiais, has also virtually disappeared as a spoken language.

ECONOMY

Guernsey saw major changes during the late 20th century as the financial services industry took over from agriculture and tourism as the mainstay of the economy. The financial sector is now completely dominant, generating around 45 percent of the island's economic output and employing over 18 percent (2021) of the island's workforce. Some of the traditional activities, such as dairy farming and fishing, still survive and recent years have seen the growth of small-scale producers including cheese-makers, organic farmers and specialist pig breeders.

The tourist industry started after World War II when curious sightseers arrived to see the relics of the German Occupation. From the 1950s it became a holiday paradise with a unique position close to France together with well-run, reasonably-priced hotels and guesthouses. Tourism reached its peak in the 1980s, then suffered a decline with competition from package holidays and low-cost carriers to the Mediterranean. A fortnight's holiday to the Channel Islands is now a thing of the past and the emphasis is on upmarket short breaks. In 2008, visitors to Guernsey increased following the publication of the novel *The Literary & Potato Peel Pie Society*, which is set on the island during the German Occupation, followed by a film version released in 2018. Unfortunately, Guernsey tourism was heavily impacted by the Covid-19 pandemic (see page 23) during the 2020/21 seasons.

HISTORY AND CULTURE

It was around 8500 BC that Guernsey became an island, cut off from the landmass of Europe by rising sea levels. Jersey was separated 2,000 years later. Given the vulnerable location of the Channel Islands it was inevitable that they became stepping stones for plundering armies on their way to new conquests. For centuries the islands were prey to scourges of nature, easy pickings for passing pirates and reluctant pawns passed between warring rulers. Reminders of the past are scattered around Guernsey, from prehistoric graves to anti-French fortifications and chilling war tunnels from the German Occupation.

EARLY HISTORY

At the august Royal Guernsey Golf Club, the archaeological equivalent of a hole-in-one was achieved in 1976 just alongside the fifth green: an array of protruding stones revealed under the gorse. Artefacts discovered at the dig date back to around 4500 BC and experts rate the site, called Les Fouaillages, as one of the oldest man-made structures ever found in Europe. Later evidence of the Neolithic culture on the islands are passage graves

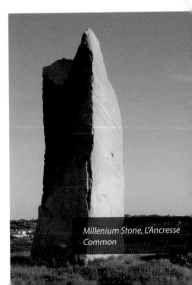

Millenium Stone, L'Ancresse Common

St Tugual Chapel

(tombs reached by tunnel), menhirs (tall monumental stones) and dolmens (stone slabs arranged as tombs). This is proof that the Neolithic residents of the Channel Islands, who lived here until around 2000 BC, had the technology to move 10-ton stones, as well as sufficient devotion to build imperishable monuments to their princes and gods.

During the Bronze and Iron ages, the Channel Islands had trade links with Britain, Ireland and France, and several sites have been discovered on Guernsey. In 1983 a rich Bronze Age site was excavated on the Hougue du Catelain at L'Ancresse, revealing large quantities of pottery, along with arrow heads, loom weights and other artefacts.

ROMANS AND CHRISTIANS

Opinion is divided whether or not the Romans colonised the islands, but they certainly passed through. In 1985 a 75ft (23-metre) -long Gallo-Roman vessel was discovered in St Peter's Port harbour. This flat-bottomed vessel, dating to around 180 AD and known to be the Roman ship 'Asterix', contained pottery, coins and a cargo of roof tiles. Castle Cornet's Maritime Museum devotes a section to the shipwreck and the preserved oak beams from the vessel will be on display in St Peter Port when a suitable site is found.

Christianity was established in the islands by the 6th century. The early Christian era was one of comparative peace, with parishes growing up around stone churches. But the peace was shattered in the 9th century when the Vikings arrived in their Scandinavian long ships, raiding the Normandy peninsula and Channel Islands. Over many years houses were burnt, islanders murdered, crops and cattle carried off and prehistoric tombs rifled. But the Norsemen were also expert sailors and farmers – skills which they left the islanders as a permanent legacy. They finally gained control of Normandy from Charles the Simple of France and in the 10th century the Duchy of Normandy expanded to the Channel Islands. The Normans made their mark here with their feudal laws, seafaring traditions and language.

THE BRITISH CONNECTION

Following the victory of Norman Duke William II (William the Conqueror) at the Battle of Hastings in 1066 the Channel Islands

INSTANT JUSTICE

For more than a thousand years any Channel Islander has been able to get what amounts to an on-the-spot injunction to stop an alleged injustice against property. The wronged party invokes the Clameur de Haro, an ancient Norman cry for help said to have been created by Rollo the Viking who was made Duke of Normandy. If a civilian feels his property is being threatened he may go down on bended knee in the presence of two witnesses, and cry: 'Haro! Haro! Haro! A l'aide, mon prince, on me fait tort' ('O Rollo! O Rollo! To my aid, my prince, I am being wronged') followed by the Lord's Prayer in French. The accused then has to await the court's ruling on whether the Clameur has been correctly raised. To this day it survives as a fully enforceable law in Guernsey and Jersey, though it is rarely invoked.

became part of the Anglo-Norman realm. This was the beginning of the link with the English Crown, reinforced in 1204 when King John lost Normandy to France. The Channel Islands were given the choice of remaining loyal to the English Crown or reverting to France. They opted for the former, and in return the king granted them 'the continuance of their ancient laws and privileges', laying the foundation for self-government. But England's hold over the islands transformed their nearest neighbour, France, into a perennial threat. Fear of invasion led to the construction of coastal fortifications and in 1204 Castle Cornet was built to command the east coast. Life under siege became so cruel that in 1483 Pope Sixtus IV issued a papal bull proclaiming the Channel Islands neutral.

At the outset of England's Civil War the town of St Peter Port and the castle that was intended to protect it were on opposite sides of the conflict. St Peter Port sided with the Parliamentarians whilst the governor of Guernsey supported the Royalist cause and holed up in Castle Cornet with his supporters. Besieged for no less than eight years, they fired some 30,000 cannon balls into Cromwell's St Peter Port.

NAVIGATION AND KNITTING

In the second half of the 17th century peace brought prosperity, which spread from the local grandees to merchants, sailors, and incipient industrialists. Privateering, whereby Channel Islands ships were licensed to capture enemy vessels and confiscate their cargoes, became a major source of revenue. As England imposed duty on imported luxury goods to fund its wars with France, Spain and the American colonies, Guernsey became a major supplier in the smuggling trade, shipping large quantities of captured bread, perfume and lace to England. This legalised piracy led to the development of a sizeable shipbuilding industry.

Meanwhile trade in wool between Southampton and the Channel Islands led to the rapid growth of the knitwear industry with the islands exporting high-quality sweaters, stockings and gloves to England and France. Knitting in fact became so popular and lucrative, with fishermen and farmers taking it up as well as women and children, that the harvest crops and seaweed collection began to suffer. A moratorium on

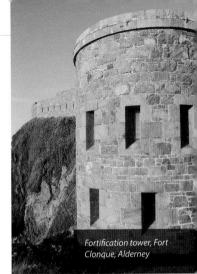

Fortification tower, Fort Clonque, Alderney

knitting was imposed forbidding the making of stockings during harvest and vraicing (seaweed collection).

Jersey's privateering activities in the 1770s led to two attempts by France to capture the island, first in 1779 and more famously in the Battle of Jersey in 1781 when the heroic Major Francis Peirson led the local militia to victory. This was the last attempt by France to capture either island. But the fear of further invasions led both Jersey and Guernsey to construct dozens of Martello towers around the coasts, many of which can be seen today.

THE VICTORIAN ERA

A period of prosperity followed the English victories at Trafalgar in 1805 and Waterloo in 1815. Retired army and navy officers began to settle on the islands, attracted by the low cost of living. But even though hostilities officially ceased after the defeat of Napoleon there was still suspicion between England and France,

Life in a Small World

If you read just one book on Guernsey make it *The Book of Ebenezer Le Page* by G.B. Edwards, the highly entertaining and moving reminiscences of an 80-year-old recluse on his life on Guernsey in the 20th century and his despair at the trappings of modernism. It was the only novel by Guernsey-born G.B. Edwards, but has received much critical acclaim since its posthumous publication.

a legacy of which are the Victorian defensive fortifications and notably Alderney's Braye Breakwater (1847–64). The intention was to convert Braye harbour into a massive naval base with a breakwater at each side of the bay. Only the western wall was built, originally a mile (1.5km) long.

Ship-owning in Jersey and Guernsey expanded rapidly in the first half of the 19th century, ranking the islands 10th among British ports in 1865, ahead even of Hull and Bristol. The growth was powered initially by oyster fishing and the cod trade, but gradually international shipping became more important, with Channel Island vessels, many of them built locally, travelling as far as Australia. But when iron steamships began to dominate the seas in the 1870s the islands were badly hit: the local ship builders couldn't afford to build them and local ship owners couldn't afford to buy them. The great seafaring days were over and the islanders turned to agriculture and tourism.

THE GERMAN OCCUPATION

The Channel Islands were the only British territory to fall into German hands during World War II. Tiny they may have been but Hitler saw them as the first step to his intended invasion of the United Kingdom. In 1940 Churchill decided that the islands, which had no strategic value for Britain, could not justify the cost of defence and the decision was taken that they should be demilitarised. This was to be part of Hitler's Atlantic Wall project, a line of defence works extending all the way from the Baltic to the Spanish frontier.

Prior to the arrival of Hitler's troops thousands of islanders, including almost the entire population of Alderney, fled to England, fearing the worst. The islands were turned into impregnable fortresses, with thousands of foreign forced labourers and Russian prisoners-of-war toiling in harsh conditions to construct concrete walls, command posts, bunkers and gun emplacements around the islands. Hitler believed that the Allies would eventually seek to retake the Channel islands and forced labourers were put to work on the German military hospital (see page 43), built underground to cater for hundreds of German casualties in the event of an attack. The allied landings never happened, the space

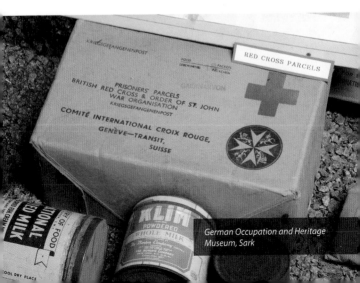

German Occupation and Heritage Museum, Sark

was used to store munitions stock-piled by the Germans, the medical equipment was removed and today it is dimly lit, dank and cavernous – a sombre memorial to the slave workers who died here.

Following the D-Day landings the supply lines used by Germans through France were cut off and both civilians and occupying soldiers suffered hardship and deprivation. During the last months the near-starving population was saved by the Swedish SS *Vega*, bringing Red Cross food parcels and other essential provisions. On 9 May 1945 British forces liberated the Channel Islands and the occupying forces surrendered peacefully. Citizens gathered to listen to Churchill's broadcast of the German capitulation: 'And our dear Channel Islands are also to be freed today.' Liberation Day on 9 May has been celebrated ever since and especially so in 2015, the 70th anniversary of Liberation.

POST WAR

At the end of the war German prisoners were put to work dismantling forests of barbed wire and digging up thousands of mines. Fortunately, the German Army had posted *Achtung!* warnings on the edge of minefields. After World War II the islands saw a boost in tourism from visitors curious to see the aftermath of the Occupation. Greenhouse horticulture thrived, peaking in the 1970s when nine million trays of tomatoes were being exported annually. Competition for the UK market however, particularly from the Dutch and Spanish, led to a dramatic decline in the industry. Since the 1980s finance has been the mainstay of the economy. Stable government and advantageous tax laws led to the development of international financial services. Tourism flourished up to the late 1980s but now accounts directly for less than three percent of GDP. Cruise ships calling in at St Peter Port have given the industry a bit of a boost, increasing the number of day visitors. The capital welcomed around 80 ships each year pre-Covid-19 pandemic.

IMPORTANT DATES

c.8500 BC Guernsey cut off from mainland France by rising sea levels at the end of the last Ice Age.

4500 BC Construction of Les Fouaillages, Guernsey, the oldest of the passage graves.

AD 556 St Sampson brings Christianity to Guernsey.

933 Channel Islands annexed to the Duchy of Normandy.

1066 William the Conqueror, 10th Duke of Normandy, conquers England and establishes the first constitutional links between Britain and the Channel Islands.

1204 King John loses Normandy to France but the islands remain loyal to the English Crown and are granted self-government.

1250 Work on Castle Cornet begins.

1564 Helier de Carteret colonises Sark, setting up the feudal system.

1651 Castle Cornet is the last loyalist stronghold in the British Isles to surrender in the Civil War.

Mid-18th century Privateering (legal piracy) becomes a major source of revenue for the island.

1900 Guernsey's parliament adopts English as its official language.

1940 Channel Islands demilitarised and thousands are evacuated.

1940–4 The Germans occupy the islands, building substantial fortifications.

1945 German forces surrender unconditionally on 9 May.

2009 In Sark the new democratic Chief Pleas (legislative body) is sworn in after 450 years of feudalism.

2015 Celebrations on all the Channel Islands mark the 70th anniversary of Liberation from German occupying forces (9 May 1945).

2016 Vice Admiral Sir Ian Corder CB is sworn in as Lieutenant Governor of the Bailiwick of Guernsey, succeeding Air Marshal Peter Walker, who died in the post.

2020 The Covid-19 pandemic, and measures taken to contain it, cause an economic downturn in Guernsey.

2022 With increased Covid-19 vaccination rates restrictions are eased and tourism returns.

St Peter Port Harbour

OUT AND ABOUT

Guernsey is a tiny island of 24 sq miles (62 sq km) miles and it is only 10 miles (16km) by road between the two furthest points on the island. Bear in mind though that journeys, particularly in built-up areas, can be very time-consuming.

Guernsey is divided up into 10 parishes, not that you would be aware which one you were in when driving around. The island is roughly triangular in shape and divides into two quite distinct parts: to the south and east is the cliff-fringed 'high parish' region where access to the beach is via deep wooded valleys or steep rock-cut steps. The 'low parish' region to the north and west of the islands consists of flat land fringed by miles of sand dunes.

Many visitors choose to stay in or close to St Peter Port, justifiably described as one of Europe's most appealing harbour towns. It is the hub of the island with the best choice of restaurants, shops and sightseeing on the island. Beach lovers and extreme sports enthusiasts should head for the west coast, fringed by fine sandy beaches; keen walkers to the south coast for 28 miles (44.5km) of footpaths along the flower-clad cliffs. The peaceful little sister islands of Herm, Sark and Alderney offer the ultimate escape from the stresses of life.

ST PETER PORT

Hugging the slopes that rise steeply back from the sea, Guernsey's captivating capital, **St Peter Port ❶**, creates

Tourist Information

A good place to begin exploring the town is the excellent Guernsey Information Centre (www. visitguernsey.com) on North Esplanade, with its informative displays and helpful staff.

a spectacular vista as you arrive by sea. Church spires and steep-roofed granite houses are stacked on the hillside while in the harbour below the forest of boat masts jostle for attention, lending the capital an almost Mediterranean air.

The discovery of a Roman wreck in the harbour in 1985 indicated that this part of Guernsey's coastline was a refuge for seamen even in ancient times. The Town Church existed as early as 1048 and a castle has stood here since 1206, though today's town is made up mainly of finely preserved late Georgian and Regency buildings.

In former times fishing was the main activity, and St Peter Port was merely a small quayside settlement. It was through privateering or licensed piracy (see page 18) that the town grew in size and wealth. Wealthy merchants built fine houses and new buildings spread up the slopes around the town and onto the plateau above. Today 'Town', as the islanders call it, is a charming centre of narrow cobbled shopping streets and thoroughfares, with tantalising glimpses of the harbour and castle.

THE WATERFRONT

The whole harbour front has been reclaimed from the sea. Originally ships would have docked right alongside the warehouses that line **Quayside** (now converted to restaurants and shops) enabling cargoes of wine, citrus fruits, spices, sugar and wool to be lifted straight from the ship's hold into the tall Dutch-style warehouses. Linking Quayside and the High Street are a number of steep lanes, called *venelles* (Guernsey-French dialect for 'little passages'). Look up as you explore them – some are roofed over using massive timbers from broken-up ships. Between Victoria (or Crown) Pier and Albert Pier lies the old harbour where yachts, fishing craft, dinghies and inter-island ferries busily cross paths and the halyards of moored yachts clink as their crews sun themselves on deck.

The less picturesque St Julian's Pier to the north was added in the 1920s to make way for cargo ships and ferries. Today high-speed catamarans sail for mainland Britain and France. At the landward end, the Travel Trident kiosk sells tickets for ferries to Herm, the diminutive car-free island which you can see in the distance. Further along the pier you can purchase ferry tickets for Sark, another popular day trip island, one step further to the southeast.

Along the Waterfront

At the landward end of St Julian's Pier is the **Liberation Monument** Ⓐ, a granite 'needle' erected in 1995 to commemorate the 50th anniversary of the island's liberation from occupying German forces on 9 May 1945. It was here that crowds of islanders greeted

Castle Cornet at night

Discovery Pass

A Discovery Pass, available at the museums, allows unlimited entry to Castle Cornet, the Guernsey Museum at Candie, Fort Grey and the German Naval Signals Headquarters, with accompanying children going free.

the British liberators after five years under German rule. On Liberation Day each year, and only on this day, the monument casts a shadow onto the plaques on the adjacent granite bench, each marking a key event of that jubilant day. The monument is designed so that the tip of the shadow reaches each plaque at the precise time of the event it commemorates. On 9 May, the anniversary of Liberation, Guernsey residents and visitors celebrate with a Calvacade, re-enactments and a host of entertainment and activities. Celebratory events throughout the Channel Islands stretch over five weeks in April and May.

A prominent landmark on The Quay is the majestic **Town Church** Ⓑ whose sturdy steeple you can see rising above the waterfront as you arrive by sea. Although the building incorporates the nave of the medieval church, much of the original fabric was damaged during the Civil War and it underwent major restoration in the 19th century. The church has served many civic purposes through the years including the storage of fire engines and guns. The stained-glass windows replace those shattered in 1944 by an American bomb intended for a suspected German submarine in the harbour.

CASTLE CORNET

Built to protect the settlement in the 13th century, **Castle Cornet** Ⓒ (www.museums.gov.gg; daily, Easter–Oct 10am–6pm, guided tours most days at 10.30am) was formerly isolated on a rocky islet, and accessible only by boat. Today you can reach it along Castle Pier (the most southerly of the piers). A great breakwater stretches beyond the castle, with a lighthouse at the far end where anglers cast their lines. A third of the way along the pier you can divert left to **Fish Quay**, where the workaday fishing boats land their catch and gulls swoop down in the hope of tasty morsels.

Enjoying fine views of neighbouring Havelet Bay and the town skyline, the castle is a delightful maze of buildings and courtyards, linked by steps and passageways, and enhanced by carefully nurtured gardens. The castle was a stronghold of the English Crown for nearly 800 years, built when King John lost Normandy to the French in 1204, then developed and expanded over the centuries. It has been a low-profile fort since 1672, when lightning touched off the ammunition stores, bringing down the towering central

View from Castle Cornet

Le Vallette Underground Military Museum

keep and killing the governor's wife and mother, and five other people. But much of the medieval military architecture is remarkably complete. The superb views from the citadel explain the presence of German gun emplacements there. The Germans occupied the castle during World War II and had to make very few modifications to fit it for modern warfare.

The monument is surprisingly big – allow plenty of time if you want to see all the specialist museums and try to time your visit to coincide with the **noon-day gun ceremony**, when two redcoats fire an artillery salute to St Peter Port. Beware the sudden roar! **The Story of Castle Cornet** in the Lower Barracks (opposite the ticket office) traces the turbulent history of the castle using a series of reconstructions, replicas, models and original artefacts. Objects displayed include the Guernsey Falcon, an artillery piece cast in 1550. There are Guernsey-themed military and RAF museums, and an absorbing **Maritime Museum** in the Upper Barracks. This starts with prehistoric trade when stone axes were bartered for grain and fish, and ends with the modern era of high-speed catamarans. One section is devoted to Asterix, a Gallo-Roman wreck which came to grief in AD 286 in the mouth of the harbour, with a video telling of its discovery and salvage in 1982. Maritime exhibits include colourful ships' figureheads, privateer licences and Victor Hugo's personal lifebelt and lifejacket – the writer was deeply interested in the question of safety at sea and commissioned his own special safety equipment.

The Guernsey History in Action Company (www.ghiac.org) re-enacts stories from Guernsey's past from Neolithic times to World War II. Performances take place most days in the castle grounds, and usually last 15–20 minutes. For performance times check their website. Look out too for outdoor theatre performances in the castle grounds in summer and other events.

LA VALETTE UNDERGROUND MILITARY MUSEUM

Just to the south, along the coastal road, is a tunnel complex built by slave labourers during the German Occupation, now occupied by **La Valette Underground Military Museum ⓓ** (www.lavalette. tk; Mar–mid-Nov daily 10am–5pm). The tunnels served as a refuelling station for U-boats, and one of the huge fuel oil storage tanks can still be seen. The museum is packed with World War I and II military and civilian memorabilia. Along with many uniforms and medals, there are World War II posters detailing the evacuation of the islands in 1940, notices to shoot locals committing larceny and a display of Red Cross food parcels delivered by the Swedish ship, the SS *Vega*, towards the end of the war when the population of the Channel Islands was close to starving. Whips and rubber truncheons bring home the brutal nature of the treatment of the slave labourers who built the tunnels.

Across the road from the museum the seafront promenade affords fine views of Castle Cornet and neighbouring islands. At low tide you can spot **La Vallette Bathing Pools**, public swimming pools since Victorian times. The first was the Horseshoe, built in 1859 with a small dressing room, then the Ladies and Gents in 1876 and the Children's pool added in 1896. The water in the pool comes directly from the sea at high tide, and the height of the walls allow a certain amount of water to remain in the pool as the tide lowers. The walls also stop an excess of seaweed or sea creatures finding their way into the pools. In its earlier years, the pools were often visited by many people of great significance, including legendary writer Victor Hugo and Renaissance painter Pierre-Auguste Renoir.

Today the areas surrounding the pools have been redeveloped to add modern facilities (www.thebathingpools.com), and the pools are in great condition continuing to offer a safe contained area for salt-water swimming suitable for the whole family.

The South Esplanade continues a short way to another tunnel: this one was built in 1861, as part of a scheme, never completed, for building a road through to Fermain Bay (see page 40). The Germans constructed several side tunnels, using Russian labourers who left their hammer and sickle symbol on the rocky roof.

Since 1967 the tunnels housed the Guernsey Aquarium, which sadly closed in 2019 due to no longer being financially viable.

The Heart of Town

Behind the Town Church **Market Square** ❼ underwent a multi-million-pound restoration and the 19th-century market is now a 21st-century shopping mall of high street names and local traders. Produce from across the island is brought to the weekly Fresh Friday market, while on Saturdays in summer the square is the venue for open-air concerts and drama.

Even if you aren't a keen shopper, it's worth exploring the maze of the Arcades to the left as you emerge from Market Street, along with the cobbled **High Street** and its extension, **Le Pollet**. The best known thoroughfares of St Peter Port, these appealing streets are always busy by day. Many of the shops along here have tall and elegant Regency, Victorian and Edwardian facades.

At the junction of High Street and Le Pollet, Smith Street leads left and uphill towards the **Royal Court House**, the former centre of island government and administration. The streets north of here (around Hospital Lane) are home to the hidden world of finance; only the gleaming brass plaques of fiduciaries and trust corporations hint at the wheelings and dealings going on inside.

CANDIE GARDENS AND GUERNSEY MUSEUM

Above the financial district the **Candie Gardens** **Ⓕ** (year-round until dusk; free) are late 19th-century pleasure gardens with wonderful views over the port and neighbouring islands. Brass bands strike up on summer Sunday afternoons at the Victorian bandstand where there is also an excellent café. Once part of a private estate, the gardens were bequeathed to the islanders in 1871 and turned into a public park. At the top stands a statue of Queen Victoria in imperial regalia with orb and sceptre. This is diplomatically separated from a more flamboyant statue of her critic, Victor

Candie Gardens

Greenhouse and ornamental gardens, Candie Gardens

Hugo, which was given to Guernsey by the French Government in thanks for the hospitality shown by the island to Hugo during his exile.

The bandstand is incorporated into the **Guernsey Museum at Candie G** (www.museums.gov.gg; daily 10am–4pm; closed Jan), devoted to the island's archaeology, history and wildlife. Exhibits in the adjacent art gallery include Rodin's bust of Victor Hugo (1883), wearing a most expressive frown and wild beard and characterful sketches by Peter de Lièvre (1812–78) of island farmers and fishermen, giving an insight into life on the island in Victorian times. The gallery's permanent collection is put away when temporary exhibitions are on show.

GUERNSEY TAPESTRY

To the south on College Street is **St James**, a deconsecrated garrison church providing Guernsey with a versatile venue for concerts, drama, lectures and exhibitions. Part of the complex is the purposebuilt Dorey Centre, housing the **Guernsey Tapestry** ❿ (www.guernseytapestry.org.gg; May–Oct Tue–Thu 10am–4pm, Nov–Apr Thu 11am–3pm). The display comprises 10 separate tapestries, each one representing a century of Guernsey's history. These accurate and meticulously worked scenes were created by the 10 Guernsey parishes to mark the new millennium and each one bears the crest of the relevant parish.

Opposite St James is the neo-Gothic bulk of Elizabeth College, founded as a school in the 16th century and rebuilt in the 1820s using the proceeds from a special tax of a shilling on every gallon of spirits sold on the island.

VICTORIAN SHOP AND PARLOUR

One of the best vantage points of St Peter Port is to be had from the top of Victor Hugo's house, one of Guernsey's star attractions. To reach the house walk up Cornet Street stopping en route at the **Victorian Shop and Parlour** ❶ at 26 Cornet Street (www.

FOREVER FRENCH

The French novelist, poet and political activist Victor Hugo (1802–85) was granted Guernsey citizenship, but he never learned to speak English. 'When England wants to chat with me', he used to say, 'let her learn my language'. Throughout his life his heart always belonged to France and he would tell fellow exiles 'The tear in our eyes is called France.' Hugo's exile was spent in Jersey for three years, then in Guernsey for 15. Guernsey welcomed him and he returned the affection. His book, *Les Travailleurs de la Mer (The Toilers of the Sea)* is dedicated to 'the rock of hospitality and freedom... the island of Guernsey, severe and gentle'.

nationaltrust.gg/places/victorian-shop-parlour; Easter–Sept Mon–Sat 10am–4pm, limited opening during Dec for Christmas shopping; free). This well-preserved, quaint townhouse has a reconstituted parlour at the rear and a shop where volunteers in period costume sell traditional toys, souvenirs and sweets in glass jars which are measured in ounces and pounds. The building serves as the headquarters of the National Trust of Guernsey.

VICTOR HUGO'S HOUSE

From the Victorian shop you can climb up **Hauteville**, where the increasingly large and ornamented houses and villas give some indication of the status and wealth of the people who first settled here when the area began to be developed in the 1780s. The street's most famous resident was Victor Hugo, the great French

THE NATIONAL TRUST OF GUERNSEY
RESTORED THIS HOUSE IN 1987

Cornet ·26· Street

Victorian shop and parlour

romantic poet, writer and politician who lived for 15 years at No. 38, **Hauteville House ❶** (tel: 01481-721 911; www.museums.gov. gg/hauteville; July & Aug Tue–Fri, guided tours by appointment only, in English, French and German).

Hugo was more than a little eccentric, and the house, owned by the city of Paris, is a physical manifestation of his quirky ideas about monarchy, history and patriarchy. Having been thrown out of France, branded as a dangerous radical for his opposition to the *coup d'état* staged by Prince Louis Napoleon in 1851, Hugo first settled in Jersey, where he kept up a tirade against *'Napoléon le petit'* as he styled the French emperor, through his newspaper, *L'Homme*. In the same paper, he criticised Queen Victoria for making a state visit to Paris in 1855. This so angered the people of Jersey that Hugo was expelled once again – this time moving a short distance north to the island of Guernsey. Here he installed his wife (*'Madame, la mère de mes enfants'*) and family at Hauteville House, and Juliette Drouet, his mistress (*'Madame, mon amie'*) at No. 20 Hauteville, which had been his first Guernsey home. This was sufficiently close for Hugo to signal to his mistress from his bedroom window.

Whilst living here Hugo wrote some of his best-selling novels, including *Les Misérables* and *Les Travailleurs de la Mer (The Toilers of the Sea)* which is set in and around Guernsey and demonstrates Hugo's intimate knowledge of the island. Growing wealthy for the first time, Hugo indulged his taste for woodworking and interior decoration. He bought chests and pews and broke them up to line the walls and ceilings of his rooms, adding his own embellishments and VH initials to create a house that is dark, brooding, lavishly decorated and full of symbolic meaning. Significantly, he chose to write his powerfully romantic novels in a room that was, by contrast with the rest of the house, flooded with light – he constructed a rooftop observatory of glass, with far-reaching views

Sausmarez Manor Farmers' Market

over the blue seas to his beloved France.

You can view the building on a conducted tour, though the eminently knowledgeable guides make this one of the best places you can visit anywhere on the Channel Islands.

In the garden, now restored, Hugo planted an acorn for a tree which, ahead of his era, he christened 'the oak of the United States of Europe'.

SOUTHERN GUERNSEY

The south coast, where steep granite cliffs tower above secluded little bays, couldn't be more of a contrast to the flat beaches of the west. Footpaths run all the way along the cliffs, dipping down to tiny coves where the retreating tide reveals sandy beaches, some only accessible by foot. The walk along here is the most exhilarating and spectacular of the island. There is plenty for sightseers too, with a fine old manor house and gardens, German Occupation museums and 'the smallest chapel in the world'.

SAUSMAREZ MANOR

South of St Peter Port, off the Sausmarez Road, lies the stronghold of one of Guernsey's oldest families: **Sausmarez Manor** ❷ (www.sausmarezmanor.co.uk; grounds daily 10am–5pm, free apart from Subtropical Gardens and Art Park; house tours June–Sept

Mon–Thu 10.30am, 11.30am and 2.30pm, first half Apr and second half of Oct Mon–Thu 11.30am, mid-Apr–May and first half of Oct Mon–Thu 10.30am and 11.30am). The de Sausmarez family have lived here since 1254, and a fine series of family portraits hangs in the imposing grey granite house, which dates from 1714. The family has been one of Guernsey's most distinguished dynasties, having served as bailiffs, governors, naval officers and diplomats. The manor is still lived in and you may well come across the Seigneur, Peter de Sausmarez, chatting to visitors. He also takes the evening Ghost Tours.

Manor Gardens

Surrounding the house are delightfully informal gardens, where you might possibly trip over free-range ducks and hens scrabbling for food in the undergrowth. Attractions include a **pitch-and-putt course**, a **Coppersmiths' Workshop** in the Tudor Barn where the craftsman is the only surviving coppersmith to make the traditional Guernsey milk cans in the time-honoured way, a **ride-on 7¼-gauge trains** and children's play area, a craft shop and a tearoom in the old vinery by the lakeside, and a gallery with gifts and home furnishings. Don't miss the **Sculpture Park**, one of the largest and most varied in Britain, set amid subtropical woodland. Showing around 220 works by 90 artists, this is a fascinating collection, from life-size figures to flying frogs, with a surprise around every corner.

If you happen to be here on a Saturday you're in for a treat. The **Farmers' Market** is held in the grounds from 9am–noon (Nov–Apr) and has a wonderful range of local produce: chancre and spider crabs, local beef and pork, free-range eggs, cheeses, Guernsey *gâche* (fruit loaf) and home-made cakes and pies. You will also find handmade arts and crafts, bric-à-brac, jewellery, antiques and plants.

FERMAIN BAY

East of Sausmarez Manor lies one of Guernsey's prettiest beaches, **Fermain Bay ❸**. Bobbing with boats and washed by gentle waves, the bay has the air of the Mediterranean. This is a lovely spot for sunbathing, swimming in the sparkling waters (though sand is only exposed at low tide) and diving from the steps. Despite being one of Guernsey's most picturesque spots, the bay is rarely crowded since the only vehicular access is by a private road, closed to all but permit holders, and there is no nearby parking. This does not put off the punters coming by day or evening to the Fermain Beach Café, one of Guernsey's top café/restaurants and an ideal spot for a break.

JERBOURG POINT

On the southeast corner of the island **Jerbourg Point ❹** has the most compelling views on the south coast. With good visibility you can see Jersey to the south, the other Channel Islands to the east, and the coast of Normandy beyond. From the most southerly tip of the point you can see six rock formations known as the Pea Stacks of the East or **Les Tas de Pois d'Amont**. The rocks look like monks (especially from a boat), with stooped backs and deep pointed hoods – particularly the middle stack, which is known as Le Petit Bonhomme d'Andriou (The Little Good Man Andrew). The story goes that Andriou, a pagan priest, witnessed a ship heading for the rocks in a storm and prayed to his gods to calm the waves. The weather only worsened so he then beseeched the Christian God, vowing to become a Christian if his prayers were answered. The ship was saved, Andriou was baptised and built a chapel on the site. In bygone days sailors used to pay their respects as they sailed past Andriou. Today the stacks are a habitat for nesting birds.

The cliff path which you can pick up on the Jerbourg peninsula goes all the way west to Pleinmont (see page 48).

MOULIN HUET BAY

A steep path near Doyle's Monument leads down to **Petit Port** ❺. This is one of Guernsey's loveliest beaches and when the tide rolls out to reveal the sandy expanse, it's a perfect spot for bathing, provided you don't mind the return climb up 270 steps! The cliff path westwards from Petit Port leads to the gorgeous **Moulin Huet Bay** ❻. If going by car, follow the signs from the main road after Sausmarez Manor, then it's a 5-minute walk down a steep path. With its striking rock formations, caves and waterfall, the bay is best enjoyed when the water is at half-tide or below, as the loveliest bits are covered by water at high tide. The French Impressionist painter, Pierre-Auguste Renoir, was so captivated by the bay's rock pools, cliffs and sea caves he painted no fewer than 15 pictures of the scenic cove on a painting trip to Guernsey in 1883.

Moulin Huet Bay

LA GRAN'MÈRE DE CHIMQUIÈRE

Guernsey's most appealing piece of prehistory stands in the most unlikely spot for a pagan monument: at the entrance to the graveyard of St Martin's Church. This is in the village of St Martin a short way inland from the coast. The **Gran'mère de Chimquière** ❼ (Grandmother of the Cemetery) is considerably older than most grandmothers and though stony faced she nevertheless flaunts her naked breasts. She was carved in the early Bronze Age, possibly 4,000 years ago and modified to represent a Mother Goddess about 2,000 years later. If you visit after a wedding Gran'mère is quite likely to be wearing a garland of flowers: newlyweds traditionally place flowers on her head for luck. The crack through the torso is believed to have been the result of an attack by a church warden who was angry over the worshipping of stone idols.

Pea Stacks and Jerbourg Point

GERMAN UNDERGROUND MILITARY HOSPITAL

From St Martin's take the main road going west, signed to the airport, and in just over half a mile (0.8km) turn right following signs for the **German Underground Military Hospital** ❽ (www.germanundergroundhospital.co.uk; Apr–Oct Fri–Mon 10am–4pm).

Gran'mère de Chimquière

Tucked away down a green lane, this is one of the largest complexes in the Channel Islands constructed during the Occupation era. The hospital is a testimony to Hitler's mistaken belief that the Allies would, as a matter of pride, eventually seek to attack and retake the Channel Islands. Hitler entrusted the task of fortifying the islands to Dr Fritz Todt, who had earlier been responsible for planning and building Germany's *autobahn* system. Organisation Todt, as it was known, involved turning the Channel Islands into an impregnable fortress, with artillery able to cover a whole sweep of the French coast.

This hospital, along with its counterpart in Jersey, was intended for the treatment of hundreds of German military casualties in the event of an attack. Built underground, the wards and operating theatres were hewn out of solid rock by slave workers from Russia, Poland, Alsace and the Czech Republic, many of whom died as a result of the brutal treatment meted out by the German occupying forces.

The tunnels took more than three and a half years to build but were operational for only nine months. The expected Allied

German Underground Military Hospital

invasion never came and the occupying forces surrendered on 9 May 1945. Instead, the space was used principally to store the vast quantities of munitions stock-piled by the Germans.

Nearly all the military medical equipment was removed and as a result the Hospital is sombre and cavernous. Unlike its counterpart in Jersey there are only a handful of displays, and the dim lighting, damp concrete floors and the very emptiness of the place render it a chilling reminder of Guernsey under the jackboot.

THE LITTLE CHAPEL

Just west of this dank and chilly spot lies the **Little Chapel** (www.thelittlechapel.gg; open daily; free, donations encouraged) which is both kitsch and enchanting. The building is a complete church in miniature, and claims to be the smallest in the world. The chapel is modelled on the grotto in the Church of Lourdes and every square inch is encrusted with seashells, coloured pebbles and china and glass fragments. Barely 16ft (5 metres) in length, the chapel has difficulty accommodating even a dozen people. It is the third in a series of mini-chapels built on the site by a monk, Brother Deodat, in 1923–39 (a fellow monk added final touches in the years to 1965).

PETIT BÔT BAY

Back on the south coast some of the island's most attractive 'water lanes' (or lush valleys) run down to **Petit Bôt Bay** ⑩. This attractive cove is a popular bathing spot, and one of the island's sunniest and most sheltered bays. Arrive early as parking space is limited. A Napoleonic-era loophole tower stands guard over the bay, and what was once an old mill is now occupied by a café with a sea view. The brooks that run down the sides of the green lanes used to power two mills, one of which was used for paper-making.

GERMAN OCCUPATION MUSEUM

German bunkers and artillery lookouts are the most tangible testament to wartime days, but they convey little of life at the time. The **German Occupation Museum** ⑪ (www.germanoccupationmuseum.co.uk; daily, Apr–Oct 10am–4.30pm, Nov–Mar 10am–1pm), behind Forest Church and signed off the main road, fills the gap. This is an absorbing war museum founded in 1966

The Little Chapel

Martyn Guille

Close to the Little Chapel you'll find the Martyn Guille Gold and Silver Workshop (www.martynguille.com; Mon–Sat 9am–5pm; free), where you can watch craftsmen at work and browse the showroom. Among the items made here are the famous Guernsey milk cans, the last surviving relic of Guernsey's Norman ancestry.

by Richard Hearne who was a child during the German Occupation and still oversees the museum.

Among the many exhibits is a large painting depicting a Rhine Valley scene, complete with castle and vineyards, painted on the walls of a nearby house by a homesick soldier. Another rarity is a stone painted with a red V (for Victory) sign. Guernsey people showed their defiance by painting such signs wherever they could until the occupying troops took to painting laurel wreaths underneath to represent German victory. There are informers' letters, a horse's gas mask, some wartime condoms (German issue), a doll's house made from cardboard boxes and letters from the Controlling Committee of the States of Guernsey giving instructions for the distribution of food during the dark days towards the end of the war when food was desperately short. Surprisingly, cigarettes did not need to be rationed – experiments in growing tobacco on Guernsey proved very successful, ensuring an unlimited supply of locally made cigarettes. The reconstruction of a wartime kitchen on Guernsey, with recipes for marrow pudding and potato sponge, tell of civilian hardships. Street scenes from St Peter Port show hungry locals queueing outside the butcher's for a ration of meat in 1941.

PLEINMONT HEADLAND

The main road to the Pleinmont Headland goes takes you past **Torteval Church** with a distinctive round tower and witch's-hat spire. Standing prominently on the windy headland to the west is the **Pleinmont Observation Tower** ⑫ (Aug Sun 2–4.30pm, last entry 4pm; check with Guernsey Information Centre for other opening times), a fully-restored World War II naval observation tower, pierced by viewing slots. It was from here that German observers controlled Guernsey's coastal artillery, communicating with the gunners by radio.

On the same headland to the north is the **Table des Pions**, also known as 'The Fairy Ring', a grassy mound encircled by a ditch. This spot played a prominent role in a medieval ceremony, the *Chevauchée de St Michel*, when officers of the feudal court inspected the highways and sea defences to ensure that local landowners were fulfilling their duty to maintain them. The pions were the footmen who accompanied the officers and the Table des

Petit Bôt Bay

Pions was the spot where they took a break to enjoy an open-air banquet.

THE WEST COAST

Wide sandy beaches, where islanders come to play, are the big attractions of the west coast. Vazon Bay is a magnet for the island's extreme sports enthusiasts, luring surfers when the conditions are right, while Cobo Bay is the most popular beach for families. For diversions from the beaches there are burial chambers, coastal forts, Lihou Island (when the tide is right) and, inland, Saumarez Park.

ROCQUAINE BAY

Merging with L'Erée Bay, **Rocquaine Bay** ⑬ is over 1 mile (1.6km) long with alternating beaches and rocky outcrops. At low tide it forms one continuous stretch of sand – Guernsey's biggest

SOUTH COAST CLIFF PATH

The footpath along the south coast cliffs is the most spectacular and challenging walk on the island. It is 15 miles (24km) from St Peter Port all the way to Pleinmont Headland in the west. The walk can either be done in its entirety over a long day, or in separate shorter sections at a gentler pace. The path requires some stamina, especially for the steep climbs up and down from the bays, but you can take breaks at beachside cafés. The walk can be done at any time of year, but the scenery is at its best in spring when wildflowers carpet the cliffs and birds come ashore to nest. Don't forget to bring binoculars to spot fulmars, cormorants, shags, and the gannets and puffins that nest on offshore islets. Dolphins, grey seals and basking sharks are also occasionally spotted from the cliff paths.

Fort Grey at dusk

beach, with safe swimming and rock pools to explore. During late July to early August the beach is the main focus of the Rocquaine Regatta, a full day and evening of free entertainment and whacky events like raft racing. To the south lies **Portelet,** a quiet sandy cove at the foot of the south coast cliffs that boasts a small working harbour. If the tide is out, Portelet is a brilliant place for a swim. Alternatively, there is a prettily-sited tea garden at the top with sweeping views

FORT GREY

At the southern end of the bay, **Fort Grey** ⓮ was built in 1804 as part of Sir John Doyle's grand scheme for defending Guernsey against potential attack from Napoleon's army. With its outer curtain wall and inner tower, the fort is affectionately known as the Cup and Saucer. The excellent **Shipwreck Museum** (www.museums.gov.gg; late Apr–Oct daily 10am–4pm) is housed within the tower and could not be in a more appropriate setting: overlooking the graveyard of more than 90 recorded shipwrecks.

The treacherous rock-strewn coasts and strong currents around the Channel Islands have always posed a hazard for ships. From the earliest seafaring days two crucial trade routes passed close to Guernsey: from Britain and northern Europe to the Mediterranean and from the English Channel to America.

But it was the 19th-century surge in trade that led to the largest number of disasters. In bad weather captains would mistake the Channel Islands for the south coast of England and steer south, intending to head into the middle of the Channel but in fact aiming straight at the reefs. One of the worst disasters was the railway steamer, SS *Stella*, which ran into fog and struck the Casquets in 1898. The boat sank within eight minutes of impact, and 105 people lost their lives. Building a lighthouse on the Hanois reef in 1862 reduced the annual toll of shipwrecks, and in 1975 the shipping lane for ocean-going vessels was moved 10 miles (16km) west to avoid further casualties.

The Shipwreck Museum tells the grim story of many of the local shipwrecks and displays salvaged treasures, from a ship's bell and a fine candelabra to coffee pots from the SS *Yorouba*, which foundered in 1888.

A GUERNSEY TO WEAR

Channel Islanders have been busy knitting since the 15th century. Queen Elizabeth was in favour of Guernsey stockings and Mary Queen of Scots even wore a pair to her own execution. Knitting became so lucrative that fishermen and farmers took it up as well as women and children. While the word 'jersey' has entered the English language, the stylish Guernsey is far less well known. It was originally made for seamen, the tightly knitted stitches producing a hard-wearing garment. By the 19th century the Guernsey had become well known and Nelson adopted it as standard issue for the English navy. Today one of the few outlets where you can find Guernseys is Le Tricoteur, next to Guernsey Pearl on Rocquaine Bay. If you are wondering where the sheep are, most of the wool is imported.

Le Creux ès Faies dolmen

L'ERÉE HEADLAND

To explore the headland at the northern tip of **L'Erée Bay** take the small road left off the main coast road (after the Taste of India restaurant) which leads to the headland. Just after the German bunker there is a small sign on the right to **Le Creux ès Faies** ⓯. This is the island's third largest megalithic tomb, a dolmen which you can crawl inside. The name means 'Cave of the Fairies' as it was believed that fairies came out on moonlit nights to dance on the nearby Catioroc headland. The prehistoric passage grave was probably built around 3000 BC and used for 1,000 years or more, with bodies and ashes being placed in the chambers, along with gifts of pottery, flint and stone tools.

Beyond the dolmen stands **Fort Saumarez** ⓰, a strange feat of World War II improvisation: a four-floor observation tower tacked on to an 18th-century Martello-style tower. The fort is named after Lord James Saumarez, who in 1794 defeated five attacking French frigates with his ship, HMS *Crescent*. The head-land commands fine views of sweeping Rocquaine Bay to the south and Les Grandes Rocques to the north. A monument here commemorates those who lost their lives when MV *Prosperity* foundered on the reefs off Perelle Bay in January 1974 with the loss of all 16 crew.

LIHOU ISLAND

From the car park, a path leads down to the centuries-old cause-way, which at low tide links mainland Guernsey to **Lihou Island** ⑰. This lovely windswept islet, the most westerly point of the Channel Islands, is now a nature reserve, noted for its migrant seabirds, rab-bits, resident peacocks, sea clover and sea pinks. A notice at either end of the causeway gives the times when it may safely be crossed

View across to Lihou Island

(the tide returns swiftly, and can cut you off). You can also find the times of the tides at Fort Grey or online at www. harbours.gg and www.gov. gg/tides.

Apart from its walks and wildlife, Lihou is mainly of interest for the remains of the 12th-century Priory of St Mary, built by Benedictine monks who arrived from the Abbey of Mont St Michel in around 1114. Three dolmens and seven menhirs discovered by the monks were used as foundations for the chapel. The priory is believed to have been used until the 16th century, after which it became a farmhouse. During World War II the church was used as target practice by the Germans. Little now remains of the building, except a few wall fragments. Until 1994, when the States of Guernsey bought the island, a Guernsey law forbade all but islanders to make the crossing to Lihou.

Beyond the priory, on the northwest coast, you can climb over rocks to the **Venus Pool**, large and deep enough to bathe in, but take heed of the signs discouraging access during the nesting season.

> ### Guernsey Pearl
>
> If you visit the Guernsey Pearl jewellery shop (opposite Fort Grey) you won't find Guernsey pearls. They come from the Far East but are made up here. Visitors can watch the art of pearl stringing and purchase jewellery.

PERELLE BAY

The main road skirts the coast via L'Erée Shingle Bank towards **Perelle Bay**. At Le Catioroc, beside the Napoleonic Chinchon battery, **Le Trépied** is a prehistoric passage grave, reputed to be the place where local witches met with the devil for Friday-night revelries. Perelle Bay derives its name from the Celtic word for rock and at low tide you can see why. This used to be a favourite bay for collecting ormers, the indigenous mollusc prized for its mother-of-pearl inner shell as well as its flavour (see page 100).

ST APOLLINE'S CHAPEL

In the village of Perelle, **St Apolline's Chapel** ⑱ (open daylight hours; free), built in 1394, is a little medieval jewel, just by the road-side. It is the only chapel in the British Isles dedicated to Apolline, a deaconess martyred in 249 AD, who is regarded as the patron saint of dentistry. Fragments of frescoes depict the *Last Supper* and what is thought to be Christ washing the feet of Apostles. The chapel had been used as a cowshed before the States of Guernsey bought it in 1873 and rescued it from this humble role.

VAZON BAY

The biggest beach on the island, **Vazon Bay** ⑲ is the sports playground of the island, where Guernsey beach boys ride the rollers and shore fishermen bring in bass and mullet. To join the fun head for the Guernsey Surf School (www.guernseysurfschool.co.uk; tel: 07911-710 789) which offers coaching for all abilities and hires out wetsuits, surfboards, bodyboards and stand-up paddleboards.

FORT HOMMET

A solidly built Martello tower of red granite, **Fort Hommet** ⑳ (Apr–Oct Tue and Sat 2–4.30pm) stands on a promontory to the north of the bay and provides a panoramic view of Vazon and the whole coast. Wherever you find Napoleonic fortifications there are sure to be German defences, for the Occupation troops appreciated the skills of their predecessors in finding sites from where artillery could cover a large sweep of coast. Here, a German gun casemate has been restored as operational in 1943–5 with a full interpretation of Fort Hommet Headland.

COBO BAY

Next along is **Cobo Bay** ㉑, another fine bathing beach, particularly popular with families. As evening falls, barbecues light up along the beach, and diners gather on the terrace of the **Cobo Bay Hotel** ㉒ to watch the setting sun. The distinctive pinky-red rock along the coast here is known as Cobo granite and has long been a source of stone for buildings on the west side of the island. If you climb

Cobo Bay

the steps to the top of the now-wooded quarry behind the bay, you will find the **Rocque de Guet Watchhouse and Battery**, a Napoleonic watchtower, from where there are splendid views of Vazon, Cobo and Grandes Rocques bays.

SAUMAREZ PARK

Inland from Cobo Bay, off the Route de Cobo, is **Saumarez Park** ㉓ (daylight hours; free except when special events are held here; not to be confused with Sausmarez Manor in St Martin). With a big adventure playground, vast park, tea-rooms and a nature trail linking it to nearby Cobo Bay, the park is an ideal destination for families. Garden lovers can enjoy the formal grounds surrounding the house and the Japanese walk and garden originally planted by one of the Saumarez who had served as the British ambassador to Japan. He came back with many exotic plants – plus a Japanese carpenter and gardeners to build a Japanese temple and tend the grounds. The entire property was purchased in 1938 by the States of Guernsey, and opened to the public.

FOLK AND COSTUME MUSEUM

Within the park is the National Trust of Guernsey's **Folk and Costume Museum** (www.nationaltrust.gg/places/folk-costume-museum; early Apr–Oct daily 10am–5pm). This excellent museum, within 18th-century farm buildings grouped around a cobbled courtyard, shows life on the island as it used to be around 100 years ago. Visitors can see a reconstructed farmhouse kitchen, the town house parlour of a middle-class home and a display on childhood.

Displays in the outbuildings give an insight into the varied diet and the never-ending pattern of work involved in rural life.

Folk and Costume Museum

There are crab pots, ormering hooks, rabbit traps, pig-killing knives, carts and carriages and a Victorian mangle used by children doing the washing.

NORTHERN GUERNSEY

The grandeur of the sweeping west coast beaches gives way to smaller, more intimate bays, inlets and harbours, particularly in the northeast. The flat landscape is entirely different in character from the southern cliffs and central uplands. The west-facing coast is backed by dunes and sandy common, too poor to farm, but used as a golf course. Inland, the region is more heavily developed, with industrial complexes around St Sampson and greenhouses producing cut flowers.

Rousse Tower

AROUND LE GRAND HAVRE

Rousse Tower ㉔ (www.museums.gov.gg/towers; Apr–Oct early morning until dusk) which stands on the headland to the west of Le Grand Havre, is one of a chain of 15 loop-holed towers built in the 1780s against the threat of invasion by France. It has been fully restored and contains displays on the history of Napoleonic-era fortifications on Guernsey. Perched on a small rise and visible across the bay is **Vale Church** ㉕ a place of worship for over 1,000 years and for pagan ritual long before that. The best bets for a swim are **Les Amarreurs Harbour** ㉖, a scenic beach with a small jetty and play area, or nearby **Ladies Bay** ㉗ where the white sands are only revealed in their glory when the tides are low.

OATLANDS VILLAGE/GUERNSEY FREESIA CENTRE

South of Le Grand Havre **Oatlands Village** ㉘ (www.oatlands.gg; Mon–Fri 9.30am–5pm, Sat 10am–5, Sun noon–5pm; free entrance but charges for some activities) caters for all ages. Gift shops and craft workshops are grouped around a courtyard set in converted brickworks, complete with bottle-shaped kilns. Diverse attractions over the 5-acre (2-hectare) site include an attractively landscaped mini-golf course, a Jungle House play area with a soft play zone and eight full-size trampolines, junior go-karts, bowling alley, a large craft and hobbies shop, a *chocolatier* and a variety of eateries.

At the nearby **Guernsey Freesia Centre** ㉙ (www.freesiasbypost. com; daily 10am–5pm, closed Sun in winter; free), you can see freesias at different stages of bloom and arrange to have flowers sent to friends and family at home. Flowers are dispatched daily to the UK.

L'ANCRESSE COMMON

At the very northern end of the island, from the high points on **L'Ancresse Common** ㉚ the horizon bristles with tall circular towers and square forts, spaced at regular intervals, each one guarding

View of L'Ancresse Common

a possible landing site and intended as a show of strength to deter Napoleon from planning an invasion. Far harder to spot is the oldest prehistoric site on Guernsey (and one of the earliest in Europe) hidden among the gorse and bracken on the southern edge of the common. To locate it ask a golfer for the fifth green or take the path with a sign to the site on a boulder off Les Amarreurs Road (leading to Les Amarreurs Harbour). The history is fascinating, but the triangle of stones is unlikely to inspire unless you are an expert. Named **Les Fouaillages** **31** this roofless burial chamber was constructed more than 6,000 years ago and only rediscovered in 1976. Two mounds rise above the golfers' 17th green: a German bunker and **La Varde**, a 40ft (12-metre) passage grave, the island's largest. In the centre of the tomb a 6ft (1.8-metre) person can stand straight and examine the huge capstones.

PEMBROKE AND L'ANCRESSE BAYS

At the north of the island the adjoining **Pembroke and L'Ancresse Bays** **32** form one huge stretch of flawless beach. With white sands, water sports and clear blue waters this is arguably the island's best though it is often windy and at low tide you might run out of steam pursuing the sea hundreds of yards down the slope of sand. There are beach cafés either end where you can sit and soak up this lovely stretch of coastline; and if it's too cool for swimming or sitting alfresco there are footpaths in either direction for a bracing walk.

The island's northern road then fringes the common and turns south. From here on, the beaches are subject to fast currents and more suited to rockpooling and birdwatching.

NORTHEAST COAST

The northeastern corner of the island is defended by the 19th-century **Fort Doyle**, truncated and modernised by the Germans.

More modernity can be found in the sleek yachts at **Beaucette Marina 33** an all-weather harbour blasted out of the island's bedrock. Guernsey's most atmospheric passage grave is **Le Déhus Dolmen 34** (daily 9am–sunset; free) under a grassy mound right by the roadside opposite glasshouses. Not only is the dolmen perfectly preserved, with a small wooden door for an entrance, it is also dramatically lit. Look carefully and you can see a mysterious carving on one of the tomb's massive capstones: the figure of a bearded man, armed with bow and arrows, known as the Guardian of Le Déhus. The large quantity of artefacts discovered here are now in St Peter Port's Guernsey Museum.

BORDEAUX HARBOUR

Old-fashioned in comparison to Beaucette Marina, **Bordeaux Harbour 35** has offered anchorage to a local fleet of boats since the Middle Ages. It's popular with fishermen and birdwatchers, and is a pleasant spot for picnics with uninterrupted views towards the islands of Herm and Sark. To the south it is overlooked by the

BECOMING A LOCAL

If you fall in love with Guernsey, and fancy living here, you will need deep pockets. A glance at any estate agent's window will reveal that there are two types of property on the market: reasonably priced accommodation and the phenomenally expensive. One two-bedroom apartment may be priced at £350,000, whilst its identical neighbour costs £1 million. The reason is that the cheaper apartment can only be bought by a Guernsey native, whilst the millionaire's property is for sale on the open market. By this means Guernsey controls migration to the islands, which would otherwise be flooded by tax exiles.

hilltop relics of the medieval **Vale Castle**, thought to have been built on an Iron Age fort.

ST SAMPSON

The second harbour of Guernsey, the town was named after **St Sampson** who was born in Wales and moved to Brittany where he founded a monastery and became Bishop of Dol in around AD 550. He travelled from Brittany to Guernsey and is believed to have landed in the natural harbour that now bears his name. He brought Christianity to Guernsey and is said to have founded a chapel where the parish church of St Sampson now stands. Today's church was built in 1111, and originally stood on the seashore.

The former industrial hub of the island, the town has been spruced up and is home to a well-equipped modern marina. But it is still a commercial working harbour with shipyards, power station and oil tankers, and given the appeal of St Peter Port just down the road there is not a lot to detain the tourist. The main port of call for shoppers is **Ray & Scott** jewellers who specialise in diamonds and have their own diamond museum (www.rayandscott.com; Museum: Mon–Fri 9am–4pm).

HERM

This diminutive island with enticing beaches and no cars makes a wonderful day or half-day trip from Guernsey. It is just 1.5 miles (2.5km) long and 0.5-miles (0.8km) wide, with a population of 66, plus a dozen Guernsey cows. You can't own a house on Herm, play a radio in public areas or pick the flowers; and the only vehicles are those used by residents for essential business purposes. Visitors come to this little paradise for the scenery, the swimming, the walking and the birdlife. It's also a favourite of foodies who come over from Guernsey for lunch or on the early evening boat

Shell Beach, Herm

to enjoy freshly caught lobster or Herm-farmed oysters. The best way to enjoy all this peace is to walk around the island. Unlike the other islands bikes (as well as cars) are banned on Herm, except for local children.

Ferries take 20 minutes from St Peter Port and usually depart eight times a day in July and August, with a reduced service off-season. Tickets can be bought from the Travel Trident Ferries kiosk on the harbour (www.traveltrident.com) or online at www.herm.com.

HERM HARBOUR

At high tide ferries dock in **Herm harbour** ㊱, while at low water passengers disembark at the Rosaire Steps before making their way along the track to the harbour. The long-established **White House Hotel** ㊲, overlooking gardens and beach, is a country house hotel with an old-fashioned charm and sense of decorum. A stay here is an escape from the 21st century – there are no televisions or telephones in the bedrooms and no clocks on the walls. Drunken quarrymen used to be incarcerated in the tiny gaol by the hotel's tennis courts, said to be Britain's smallest gaol. Any troublemakers today are shipped back to Guernsey and the prison is used to store lawnmowers.

The path going north passes the **Mermaid Tavern** (see page 112), the social hub of the island. Beyond it, **Fisherman's Beach** at low tide reveals weed-covered crates in which Herm's oysters are grown. For swimming and sunbathing there are better beaches on the east side of the island. The first main landmark on the northwards route is a tiny **cemetery** containing two graves and an almost indecipherable inscription; local legend has it that this is the grave of a mother and child who died of cholera in the early 19th century, buried here by the crew of a passing ship.

HERM COMMON

In the north of the island Herm Common has over 450 species of wild flowers, among them prickly burnet roses, sea holly, foxglove and wild thyme. Neolithic tombs, often indistinguishable from natural scatters of rock, lie scattered around the common. The needle-shaped monument at the northernmost point of the

Waiting for the ferry on Herm Island

island marks the position of one of the island's more famous dolmens, called the **Pierre aux Rats**. When quarrymen destroyed the massive grave, the local seamen were incensed at the loss of such an important landmark and navigational aid, so the obelisk was erected in its place.

SHELL BEACH AND BELVOIR BAY

Along the northeast coast lies the dazzling white, Caribbean-like expanse of **Shell Beach** ③⑧. It consists almost entirely of shells, though most have been pulverised to fragments of sand by centuries of wave action. Each tide brings in a new crop of delicate pink, yellow and luminescent shells to keep beachcombers happy. As you explore, however, you will discover that Shell Beach is by no means unique: all the island's beaches have a large amount of shells, as does the island soil.

Further south **Belvoir Bay** has a smaller but more sheltered beach, and has lovely views of Sark and (on a clear day) France. It is perfect for swimming, with crystal clear water, but the sands can get crowded in summer.

POST-WAR HERM

During World War II, the island escaped fortification, and was largely left to decay, so that the first post-war tenant spent a small fortune restoring the island farms. Even so, much remained to be done when Peter and Jenny Wood became tenants in 1949. The story of how they fell in love with Herm and worked to create the thriving but unspoilt island of today, based on the twin pillars of tourism and farming, is told in the late Jenny Wood's delightful book, *Herm, Our Island Home*, available from the gift shop at Herm Harbour.

SOUTHERN CLIFFS

From Belvoir Bay a path heads south along the undulating (and at times steep) cliff path, which encircles the island and gives access to some excellent bird-watching points. The best times are the spring and autumn migration periods, when the Channel Islands serve as a feeding ground for birds of passage. The cliffs attract nesting puffins and fulmars. In spring and early summer you can take a

Mouisonniere Beach

two-hour puffin-watching kayak tour (www.outdoorguernsey.gg/puffin-patrol) starting at Shell Beach, led by expert kayak instructors who are very knowledgeable about the puffins' routines.

Also keep an eye out for the grey seals and bottlenose and common dolphins that have made their home in the northern rocky outcrop called The Humps.

LE MANOIR

An alternative to going south along the cliff path is to head up the steep track to the huddle of granite houses at the centre of the island on the brow of the hill. Le Manoir is the village where the islanders live. Here there is an unobtrusive power station, a workshop, cottages, primary school, and the tenant's home. What appears to be a medieval keep was built in the 19th century by Prince Blücher von Wahlstatt, a wealthy and eccentric German aristocrat. He fell in love with the place in 1890 and bought the island lease. The prince introduced many trees to the island along with a colony of wallabies, which bred successfully but have since vanished.

A subsequent tenant of the island was the novelist, Sir Compton Mackenzie, best remembered for Whisky Galore (1928), who lived here from 1920 until he retired to the neighbouring island of Jethou.

ST TUGUAL

The enchanting little Norman chapel dedicated to the enigmatic St Tugual has a pint-sized bell-tower and a pretty garden with a memorial to Peter and Jenny Wood, former tenants of the island (see page 64). Rumour has it that the saint was a Welsh woman who accompanied St Magloire to Guernsey and Herm in the 6th

St Tugual Chapel

century, and her memory was perpetuated by the building of the shrine. The Wood family restored the chapel and it is used for a service most Sundays.

SARK

Victor Hugo considered Sark to be *'la plus belle'* of the Channel Islands. It is still a peaceful little island, remaining in its famous time-warp, with the atmosphere of Victorian England. The island has a population of 500 (2020) and the head of its government (or Chief Pleas) holds the ancient feudal title of Seigneur. There are no tarmac roads and the only motorized vehicles are the tractors, the ambulance and four-wheel mobility scooters.

Sark's constitution dates back to 1563, when Helier de Carteret was granted sovereignty over the island in return for maintaining a militia, whose chief task was to keep the island free of the pirates who had been using Sark as a base from which to harass English shipping. Helier took 40 Jerseymen with him to colonise the uninhabited island. He divided Sark into 40 parcels of land and granted perpetual tenancy to the occupants in return for their help in defending the island. These tenements, as they are known, have remained virtually unchanged. The feudal form of government set up in Elizabeth I's reign prevailed right up until 2008 when the island held its first general election and Sark became Europe's newest democracy.

FERRIES TO SARK

Ferries to the island are run by the Isle of Sark Shipping Company (www.sarkshipping.gg, tel: 01481-724 059) and depart from St Peter Port on Guernsey, with several sailings a day in season. The crossing time is around 55 minutes. Book ahead in the summer months when Sark is very popular with families. If you decide to

Long-lining a horse through Sark's lanes

stay on the island there are hotels, guest houses or self-catering options.

BRECQHOU AND THE BARCLAY BROTHERS

The ferry passes south of Herm before swinging northwards past the rocky islet of **Brecqhou** ㊴. This island's tenement was sold by Dame Sybil Hathaway, the most famous ruler of Sark, in 1929 for £3,000 and purchased in 1993 for a reputed £2 million as a private tax haven by the reclusive billionaire Barclay brothers, best known as owners of the Telegraph Media Group and The Ritz. The tycoon twins created a massive mock-Gothic castle on the island, complete with walls, turrets and a helipad. You can't miss it as the ferry swings to the north of Sark.

In 2008, against the wishes of the majority of the islanders, the brothers instigated the first full election on Sark. Up until then the Chief Pleas (Sark's government) had mainly comprised members who had inherited their seats under the island's 450-year-old feudal system of government. When the majority of voters rejected the Barclay brothers' preferred candidates and their manager in Sark lost his seat in the new Chief Pleas office, they withdrew their £5-million annual investment in Sark and temporarily closed down their businesses on Sark including two hotels, a pub and shops, and over 100 Sark workers were laid off.

The bitter feud continued on. The Barclay brothers owned around a quarter of Sark and they continued to seek the full de-feudalisation of the island. In 2012 the UK Minister of State for Justice, Lord McNally, informed the brothers that the UK would not let them turn the tiny island into a 'company town'. In 2015 the brothers announced the permanent closure of all four of their hotels and other holiday businesses in Sark for the

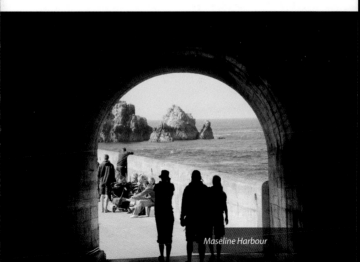

Maseline Harbour

foreseeable future. One of the twins, Sir David Barclay, passed away January 2021.

ARRIVAL IN SARK

The ferry comes in close beneath Sark's towering cliffs, past rocks where cormorants and shags launch themselves on fishing flights. At **Maseline Harbour** ⓐ ferries are met by a team of carters who take passengers' luggage to their accommodation. Sark's pettiest port, backed by a tiny shingle beach, is **Creux Harbour**, to the south, linked by tunnels through the cliffs and dotted with colourful fishing boats and smart yachts.

To reach the main village, you can either hop on the 'toast rack' – an open-sided tractor-drawn cart, which makes light of the short but steep haul up Harbour Hill – or take the pretty woodland

WILD SARK

Sark's isolated position brings a wealth of wildlife. Among the species you are likely to see along the rugged coast are puffins, shags, guillemots, razorbills and oyster catchers. For the best sitings bring your binoculars and take a two and half hour trip around the island with local fisherman, George Guille (tel: 7911 764 246). You will sail past spectacular rock formations and visit caves with deep clear water, secret beaches and coves that are only accessible by sea. Trips must be pre-booked.

One of Sark's many ancient laws forbids the shooting of seagulls, because of the guidance the birds' cries gave mariners when the wind dropped and their nesting rocks and headlands vanished into sudden sea mists. Until the mid-19th century, when it was finally conceded that another war with France was unlikely, the way into Sark's harbours was a closely guarded secret.

footpath which runs alongside the road. The morning arrival of a flood of day trippers can mar this paradise, but if you head away from the village, tranquillity is assured.

GETTING AROUND

Sark is so small you can explore it by bike in a day, preferably with a map. Bikes can be hired cheaply from Avenue Cycle Hire on The Avenue (www.avenue-cyclessark.com). In season

St Peter's Church

it's best to book in advance. There are some steep hills but pedalling is otherwise easy going. To explore some of the bays and rocky shores you have to leave the bike (no need to lock up) and continue on foot. If you're scrambling around the coastline do be aware of the state of the tide.

For the less energetic there are Sark's famous horse-drawn carriages which wait patiently at the top of the hill to take visitors on tours (approximately £15 per person for an hour). There are now more than 70 tractors, which are used for agricultural purposes, cargo deliveries and by the doctor. The ambulance is still the back end of a conventional ambulance, towed by a tractor.

BIG SARK

Sark's main road, **The Avenue**, is lined by souvenir shops, grocery stores, bike-hire outlets and café/bistros that are open all day. Note that although there is a bank, Sark has no ATMs. Most of the shops and restaurants take credit and debit cards, and some operate a cash-back system for up to £50. At the far end, beside the tourist information office, is the two-cell island prison, built to hold drunken quarry workers. Today the Sarkese locals are elected by the Chief Pleas to become the Connétable (special constable) who oversees the gaol.

The nearby **St Peter's Church**, built in 1820, has a pew reserved for prisoners, identifiable by a crossed keys design on the cushion covers. The simple building has stained-glass windows of various saints, including St Magloire, who came from Dol in Brittany in 565 to found a monastery on Sark. The monastery flourished, supporting 62 monks and serving as a school for the children of the Breton nobility, until marauding Viking pirates destroyed the buildings and killed the monks.

Continuing north you pass a stone building which houses the **Assembly Room** where the Chief Pleas' meetings take place four times a year. Sark's feudal state came to an end in 2008 when the Chief Pleas was reformed and Sark held its first election. Although Sark is no longer a feudal state and the powers of the Seigneur are much eroded, he still holds the island in perpetuity for the Crown, sits in the Court of Chief Pleas and pays the Queen an annual rent of £1.79.

LA SEIGNEURIE GARDENS

A little further north, you will be sharing the road with horses and carriages heading to and from **La Seigneurie Gardens** ㊶ (www. laseigneuriegardens.com; Easter–Oct daily 9am–6pm; donations requested; booking essential email: gardens@laseigneuriedesercq. uk).

The sheltered **walled gardens** are packed with colourful flowers and shrubs, including climbing roses and exotic plants such as the Australian Bottlebrush and New Zealand Tea Tree that flourish in the frost-free island environment. Beyond the walled garden are fruit and vegetables, which supply the on-site brasserie and a Sensory Garden whose medicinal, scented and edible plants are aimed to stimulate all five senses. The house itself (not open to the public) is no less exotic than the gardens, with the Dutch gables of its Victorian wing added to the original house of 1732 and a large watchtower built, so it is said, for sending signals to Guernsey in 1854.

Displays in the renovated chapel tell the history of Sark's Seigneurs and the Seigneurie. To the rear of the house is the Battery, where a cider apple crusher and several historic cannons are displayed alongside an ornate tower, and a turreted 18th-century dovecote. Until relatively recently one of the Seigneur's sole privileges was to keep pigeons and doves, which fed freely and with impunity on the crops of the tenants.

Point Robert Lighthouse

AROUND THE ISLAND

Sark comes into its element when you leave the village, with glorious countryside and sheer cliffs almost everywhere you go. Most of the beaches entail an adventurous scramble down the hillside – tricky if you have a bike, but it's all part of the Sark experience.

PORT DU MOULIN AND LIGHTHOUSE

A short way along the track north of La Seigneurie is a left turn that leads down through woods to **Port du Moulin** (once the site of a watermill), with fine coastal scenery. Just before you get to the beach, look out for the artificial 'Window in the Rock', a square hole perhaps cut through the cliff to allow carts to descend to the beach and gather *vraic*, or seaweed, used for fertilising the Seigneur's fields and garden. At the northern tip of the island **L'Eperquerie Common**, is named after the poles *(perques)* once erected here for drying fish.

On the east coast Sark's **lighthouse** was built in 1912 and automated in 1993. It stands halfway down the cliff into which it nestles and its platform, accessed via a flight of 165 steps, offers superb views of Maseline Harbour. On a clear day you can see all the way to France.

In Sark's southeast corner lie the best beaches and some splendid cliff scenery from the spectacular rocky spines of the Hog's Back and Pointe Derrible. **Dixcart Bay**, a fine sandy spot for bathing when the tide is out, is reached via Stocks Hotel, along a beautiful woodland path leading to the valley bottom.

On the west side of the island the **Pilcher**

Gold Post Box

Sark's only post box was painted gold in 2012 to celebrate local resident Carl Hester's gold medal win for his part in the British Olympic Dressage team.

La Coupée

Monument, on the high cliffs above the harbour of Havre Gosselin, commemorates Joseph Pilcher, a London merchant who lost his life with four others while sailing to Guernsey in a storm in 1868. This was just one of many shipwrecks.

LA COUPÉE

The vertiginous land bridge known as **La Coupée** 42 links Big Sark and Little Sark and is Sark's most famous landmark. A roadway tops the knife-edge ridge, some 10ft (3 metres) wide – you can easily take a bike across but a notice warns cyclists to dismount while crossing. To either side there is an almost sheer drop of 260ft (80 metres) straight to the sea. Crossing La Coupée was once extremely hazardous and schoolchildren had to crawl across the causeway in high winds, but the path was made good with concrete and handrails in 1945 by German prisoners of war. The steep flight of steps leading down from the north end of La Coupée to the lovely **Grand Grève** beach on the right was closed after a landslide in 2010. Two years on, the steps were repaired by volunteers and the fabulous bay is once again accessible.

LITTLE SARK

Beyond La Coupée **Little Sark** is even more peaceful than the main island. Enjoy the views of neighbouring islands as you follow the sunken lane to La Sablonnerie, a charming hotel with restaurant and tea gardens. A left turn here brings you to the tall granite chimney pots and ruins of Sark's **silver mines**, growing out of the wild bracken and brambles. Silver and copper were discovered on Sark in the 1830s and Cornish miners were brought over to work it. But no viable quantities were found, ten miners were drowned in 1845, and two years later, when the galleries collapsed and flooded, the ill-fated mining company went bankrupt.

Few make it as far as the southern tip of Little Sark and **Venus Pool**, a large natural rock pool at the base of the nearby cliffs. The 10ft (3-metre) -deep pool is uncovered for 2.5 hours either side of a low tide and visitors frequently fail to find it (ask locally about the tides and check the way). When the grass runs out and gives way to bare granite, cairns mark the best route. Reaching the pool involves a scramble, but it's a lovely spot to swim.

ALDERNEY

The island of Alderney has largely escaped mainstream tourism and remains quiet and unspoilt, with a friendly and relaxed atmosphere and a refreshing lack of bureaucracy. It certainly feels very different from Jersey or Guernsey – it is much more sparsely populated and feels quite remote even though it is only 8 miles (13km) from France. Despite its small size (3.5 miles/5.5km x 1.5

miles/2.5km) there are many miles of footpaths around the island, making it a haven for walkers and birdwatchers.

Visitors also come for the fine sandy beaches, the sailing, the restaurants and the watering holes. The islanders have a reputation for conviviality and there is a definite emphasis on taking time out to eat, drink and be merry. If you're tired of walking Alderney's wind-blasted cliffs in a squall, sitting in a

> **The Alderney Spike Girls**
>
> The distinctive blonde hedgehog is extremely rare but on little Alderney there is a thriving population. The creamy-coloured flea-free creatures, with beady button-black eyes, have a rare recessive gene. They have been breeding here since a couple of them were released in the 1960s – allegedly from a Harrods shopping bag.

warm pub is the best thing to do. The pubs are more like clubs – full of character and characters, and the natural place to be on an island that offers few places of entertainment. Alderney stole a march on Guernsey by being the first to allow publicans to open on Sundays.

Alderney's character differs somewhat from the other islands, partly because it was deliberately depopulated during World War II and used as a forced labour camp. The island was massively fortified by the Germans; relics of the Occupation can be seen along the coastline.

There are cars to hire and organised island tours but the island is best suited to those who like getting around by pedal power or on foot. A hiker can circle the island in a day.

ST ANNE

Just a few minutes' walk from **Alderney Airport** ㊸, the island's capital. **St Anne** ㊹ (referred to by locals simply as 'town') is an

Alderney Society Museum

attractive maze of cobbled streets and pastel-coloured houses.
Victoria Street is the main shopping street, with some delightfully
quirky little shops. **The Alderney Visitor and Wildlife Information
Centre** is a good source of information on island walks. Just to the
south the Victorian **St Anne's Church**, designed by Sir George
Gibert Scott, is so big that it's known as 'the Cathedral of the
Channel Islands'.

Alderney Society Museum

In the High Street, perpendicular to Victoria Street, the **Alderney
Society Museum** (www.alderneysociety.org; Apr–Oct Mon–Fri
10am–noon and 2.30–4.30pm, Sat–Sun 10am–noon), occupies an
18th-century schoolhouse and covers the fascinating story of this
little island from the Stone Age to World War II. Exhibits include
first-hand accounts of Nazi soldiers and the slaves transported
here from all over Europe to turn the island into an impregnable

fortress. Like all the Channel Islands Alderney has a history of ship-wrecks, and the museum displays some absorbing finds salvaged from an Elizabethan warship, *Makeshift*, which was wrecked off the coast and discovered in 1977 by a fisherman.

BRAYE HARBOUR

From the centre of St Anne's it's just a few minutes' walk down the hill to **Braye Harbour ⑮** and the great sandy sweep of **Braye Bay**. Protecting the beach and harbour is the massive **Braye Breakwater**, often pounded by heavy seas (walkers along the wall should be aware of sudden swamping by breaking waves). When the French began constructing a naval harbour at Cherbourg, alarm bells rang in the Admiralty, and the British government suddenly decided it was urgent to create two breakwaters to protect ships at Braye, as well as on Guernsey and Jersey. The intention was

FLYING TO ALDERNEY

From Guernsey the easiest, although not the cheapest, way to get to Alderney is to hop across by plane. It takes just 20 minutes and costs around £80–120 return. Aurigny Air Services (www.aurigny.com) operate a daily service to Alderney with their 19-seat aircraft. Alderney Airport, opened in 1935, was the first officially recognised airport of the Channel Islands. The small Terminal was built in the 1960s and has changed little over the years. Ferries to Alderney from Guernsey are very limited. Manche Iles Express (www.manche-iles-express.com) operates a high-speed ferry at weekends from April to September, the Little Ferry Company (www.thelittleferrycompany.com) is a seasonal inter-island ferry running twice daily and the slower Lady Maris II (www.ladymaris2alderney.com) only runs on Thursdays.

to convert Braye harbour into a huge naval base. But only the western wall was built, completed in 1847. Battered by massive waves, part of the breakwater was abandoned and now lies submerged beneath the waves.

Before the Royal Navy discovered Braye it was a busy little port, much frequented by smugglers and privateers. The cellars of the 18th century houses near the port were used for storing contraband. Today these houses are bars and restaurants.

ALDERNEY RAILWAY

The Alderney Railway (www.alderneyrailway.gg) is one of the oldest in the British Isles, constructed in the 1840s by the British government to convey stone from Mannez Quarry to build the breakwater and the forts. The first official passengers were Queen

Alderney Railway carriage

Victoria and Prince Albert, who were carried in 1854 in a horse-drawn tender. At weekends and on bank holidays in season visitors can take a trip in a diesel-powered railcar or one of two 1938 London underground carriages, from Braye Road to Mannez Station (or vice versa), a journey of 15 minutes.

THE NORTHEAST

A circular road hugs the northeast coast, forming a loop from Braye back to St Anne. **Fort Albert** is the first in the chain of 12 fortresses encircling the island, designed in the 1840s and 1850s. Most were never garrisoned and some have now been converted into private flats and holiday apartments, while others remain in a decayed and dangerous state. Fort Albert is perhaps the finest of them all, and is well positioned to defend Braye Harbour.

SAYE AND CORBLETS BAYS

North of Fort Albert Saye Bay (pronounced 'Soy') is an idyllic horseshoe-shaped white-sand beach between rocky headlands. Children love leaping off the rocks here – and in summer it's popular with campers from the campsite just over the dunes. The next beach along is the delightful **Corblets Bay**, with clean sands and shallow waters. This is the best beach on the island for surfing and body-boarding.

MANNEZ QUARRY AND LIGHTHOUSE

Evidence of quarrying activity lies all around the northeastern tip of the island at **Mannez Quarry**, close to the railway station terminus. Above the quarry stands the large and sinister naval direction-finder tower, built by the Germans and known locally as **The Odeon (daily 10am–4pm; free). Inside** there are four floors to explore with information boards. To the east the **Mannez Hide** is a secluded spot overlooking a pond with nine species of resident dragonfly. On the coast **Mannez Lighthouse** was built in 1912 to aid vessels along this treacherous stretch of coast. It now has LED lights and is controlled from Trinity House, Harwich.

AROUND LONGIS BAY

Continuing around the coast, **Longis Bay** is a broad crescent of white sand offering safe bathing and fine views. Additional shelter is provided by the massive concrete anti-tank wall that was partially constructed by the Germans. At the far end of Longis Bay, an attractive château-like building, known locally as **The Nunnery**, stands on the site of Alderney's Roman fort. Just to the north, **Longis Nature Reserve** and **Longis Pond and Hide** are favourite spots for ornithologists.

Longis Bay

SOUTH OF THE ISLAND

The south coast is mainly dramatic cliff walks, with almost sheer cliffs westward all the way to Hannaine Bay. This is Alderney at its most beautiful and ruggedly spectacular. Footpaths among thrift, sea campion and broom follow the line of the clifftops and you may see birds of prey soaring in the updraughts. Take binoculars for spectacular views of gannetries. South of the airport **Telegraph Bay** was previously a favourite retreat for swimming and sunbathing when the tide was out but the steps down fell into disrepair and the beach is sadly inaccessible.

Burhou Island

A couple of miles offshore, the tiny island of Burhou provides a refuge for breeding sea birds, including more than 120 breeding pairs of puffins. The island has a closed season from March to 1 August to avoid disturbance to breeding seabirds. Serious birdwatchers can arrange to stay overnight in a basic hut during the months that the island is open.

Rounding the headland the offshore islands of **Les Etacs** and distant **Ortac** teem with over 11,000 gannets, a colony which grew from a single pair that nested here in 1940. Boat trips are available in season. North of Hannaine Bay a causeway leads out to **Fort Clonque**, a Victorian fort that has been converted by the Landmark Trust into holiday accommodation (see page 141). You can only access the fort when the tide is out. The next fort up is **Fort Tourgis**, an extensive Victorian fortification, designed to accommodate over 300 men. During the Second World War these were adapted by the German forces. Nowadays the fort is a sanctuary for wildlife, especially kestrels and barn owls. The **Cambridge Battery** has been restored and is the only British fortification on the island which is open to the public.

Fun on the beach at Vazon Bay

THINGS TO DO

With a wide range of outdoor activities on offer, beautiful scenery and interesting wildlife, there are no shortage of things to do should you tire of Guernsey's many beaches. It's also a great place to take the kids on holiday, with plenty of child-friendly attractions.

SPORTS AND OUTDOOR PURSUITS

Spectacular cliff-top paths, beautiful bays for water sports and clear blue seas for fishing provide endless ways to enjoy the great outdoors in Guernsey. Along with established activities such as golf and sailing, sports enthusiasts can also try their hand at abseiling, coasteering and other adventure activities.

SURFING AND WINDSURFING

The rollers on Guernsey are not comparable to those on Jersey, but with the right conditions you can find surf on the island's west coast at Vazon Bay. The Guernsey Surf School which is based there (www.guernseysurfschool.co.uk) offers lessons and courses. Courses take place daily from July to September and are open to eight years and older, and they also run Summer Camps. The Sailing Trust Windsurfing (www.sailingtrust.org.gg), located on the Castle Emplacement in St Peter Port, offer windsurf lessons.

SCUBA DIVING

Conditions are good for scuba diving with clean (and cold) waters, good visibility and plentiful marine life. The Blue Dolphins Sub Aqua Club (www.bdsac.org.gg) offers a range of diving experiences, including shipwrecks. Dive Guernsey (www.diveguernsey. co.uk) organises courses to explore the reefs and caves around

Sailboats, St Peter

Sark, Herm and Alderney as well. The clear waters are also excellent for snorkelling and swimming.

SAILING

A steady breeze blows around the coast making Guernsey popular among yachting enthusiasts, but inexperienced sailors should beware of the tides and currents.

The Guernsey Sailing Trust (www.sailingtrust.org.gg) caters for all ages and offers a wide variety of courses, including dinghy, powerboat and windsurf lessons. The Guernsey Yacht Club (www.gyc.org.gg) at St Peter Port has full marina services, welcomes visiting yachtsmen and offers dinghy training and a wide range of boating activities. Skippered boat charter can be organised through Guernsey Boating (www.guernseyboating.com).

The Model Yacht Pond on Castle Emplacement in St Peter Port is ideal for model boat and yacht sailing or racing and is also used for beginners' sailing lessons.

ADVENTURE SPORTS

If you want to get the pulse racing a bit, you can abseil on the west coast as the sun sets or climb the cliffs in the morning light. Coasteering routes enable punters to experience the exhilaration of sea-level traversing, rock scrambling, kayaking, jumping and swimming in gullies and caves. You just come equipped with a swimming costume, a good pair of trainers, shorts or tracksuit, and a change of clothes for later. Outdoor Guernsey (www.outdoorguernsey.co.uk) hire out kayaks and operate sea kayak and coasteering trips on Guernsey year-round. During the summer, they also hire out kayaks on Herm. To explore the cave systems and beautiful wild coastline of Sark, contact Adventure Sark (www.adventuresark.com).

SWIMMING

Guernsey alone has 27 bays. If you're planning on spending time on the beach bear in mind the tides and the wind. Some of the pretty little bays in the south are only revealed at low tide, while

BOATS AND BIRDS

Cruising around the Guernsey coast, chartering a speed boat, spotting dolphins or seals, landing mackerel or sea bass and hopping across to islands are among the many boating options. Take a leisurely afternoon cruise around the east and south coast of Guernsey on board the Corsaire des Iles II (www.sarkshipping.gg), which captures spectacular coastline and beautiful bays whilst spotting puffins, oystercatchers, gannets, guillemots and other breeding seabirds. Representatives of Guernsey RSPB will be on board to provide a commentary, helping you to identify different bird species. Island RIB voyages (www.islandribvoyages.com) offer adrenaline-fuelled trips in rigid inflatable boats, exploring bays, caves and islands.

On Sark a boat trip is the best way to explore the rugged coast, caves and birdlife. On Alderney there are seasonal boat trips to see the puffin colony and gannetries; and from mid-March to mid-July you can join puffin-watching kayak trips from Shell Beach on Herm (www.outdoorguernsey.co.uk).

beaches in the north are exposed to chilly winds. Watch out too for incoming tides when the water gallops across the sands – Guernsey has one of the largest tidal ranges in the world. If you are used to indoor pools or swimming in the Mediterranean, the Channel Island waters will feel on the cool side. Most beachgoers do no more than paddle, leaving the seas delightfully crowd-free for serious swimmers. The beaches are washed twice daily by the tides and the waters are clear, but beware of strong currents and rip tides.

FISHING

With their varied coastlines, offshore reefs and clear waters the Channel Islands are ideal locations for sea anglers, especially from mid-summer to the end of autumn. The Bailiwick of Guernsey has about one fifth of all British shore records. Depending on the tides you could be bank fishing for turbot, bass and brill, wrecking for cod, conger and ling or reef fishing for pollack, bream or bass. Late summer or early autumn are ideal for shore fishing for bream, bass, sole, red mullet, triggerfish, plaice, wrasse, conger and garfish, while autumn to early winter is best for wrasse and mullet. Commercial operators include Out the Blue charters (www.boatfishing.net) for groups of 10–12 with a choice of wreck fishing, deep sea reef fishing, bank fishing or bass angling. Alderney has an international reputation as a shore fishing centre where record-breaking ballan wrasse and monster grey mullet are landed.

Rock pools are a haven for crabs, shrimps and devil fish. At strictly enforced times of

Fishing on the Net

For information on species you can catch in Guernsey and where and when to fish for them, visit www. micksfishing.co.uk. It also covers charter boat hire, tackle and bait shops.

the year you can seek out the ormer, valued by locals for their meat and by tourists for their fine mother-of-pearl interior shells. At very low tide you can sprinkle salt on the key-holed burrows of razor fish, wait for them to pop up (they will think the tide is in), then pull them from their holes. The clams are slightly chewy but can be delicious if cooked correctly, ideally steamed with wine, garlic and herbs. The best beaches for collect-

Gannet colony on Les Etacs

ing the clams are L'Ancresse Bay and any of the west coast beaches on a low spring tide.

WALKING

Walking opportunities are plentiful, from dramatic rugged cliffs to the leafy lanes of the interior. The most spectacular and challenging walk is the cliff path starting at St Peter Port and ending at desolate Pleinmont Point. The cliffs are around 320ft (100 metres) high and afford wonderful views of the tiny coves below and the waves crashing on to the rocks. The path dips down to villages where cafés and pubs provide happy distractions en route. The walk can either be done in its entirety over a long day, or in separate shorter sections at a gentler pace. With a local bus timetable you can work out when and where to be picked up and need not retrace your steps. The scenery is best in spring when wildflowers are in bloom and birds come ashore to nest.

An extensive programme of themed walks with accredited guides runs from April to September. Guides are enthusiastic and dedicated, and provide a remarkable range of themed walks. Information is available from the Guernsey Information Centre, which also provides a free walking app of Guernsey and details of Tasty Walks, a series of 20 self-guided walks designed for all ages and abilities, and punctuated by plenty of cafés, restaurants and beachside kiosks. The walks can be downloaded at www.visitguernsey.com; a full audio transcript is available, as are interactive maps.

During the Spring and Autumn Walking Festivals, guided walks focus on different aspects of Guernsey's natural beauty and heritage, with around 40 walks to choose from. *Walking on Guernsey* (published by Cicerone Guides) is an excellent booklet describing 25 walks on Guernsey, Alderney, Sark and Herm. The most detailed maps of the islands are the Ordnance Survey-style Bailiwick of Guernsey (1:15,000) or the Perry's official guide. When exploring the coast, watch out for extreme tidal movement, one of the largest recorded in the world. Beaches can disappear rapidly, so it's best to plan with an abundance of caution. And don't forget comfortable shoes, binoculars and sunblock.

Alderney has 50 miles (80km) of footpaths, across commons, cliffs and beaches. The Alderney

Coastal footpath near Petit

Wildlife Trust organises informative guided walks from May to September, ranging from history and heritage to bird watching and bat walks, plus useful leaflets on self-guided walks. During Alderney Wildlife Week in May guided walks explore the wide range of habitat and species on the island, including the unusual blonde hedgehogs. The small island of Sark is ideal for walking, as is its neighbouring island Herm, although there you have no other choice. Sark Guided Walks (www.sark.co.uk/sark-guided-walks-12927) offer three options led by Beth, a very informative and experienced local.

Every year adventurous locals walk all the way around Guernsey in a day for charity. It is a 48.5 mile (78-km) -hike, beginning at 5am. Visitors are welcome to take up the challenge. And for something even more challenging there is The Channel Island Way, a 110-mile (176km) walking route incorporating the best coastal walks in Jersey, Guernsey, Alderney, Sark and Herm. Serious ramblers can do the whole route in a fortnight (including the island-hops on ferries or boats). Obviously you don't have to do the whole route, nor do you have to be a super-fit walker. The routes on the main islands are divided into sections of 2–4 miles (3–6km), with a car park, bus stop and café at each end.

BIRDWATCHING

Guernsey has its own branch of the Royal Society for the Protection of Birds (RSPB), which welcomes members and non-members on their local, two-hour guided walks (for more information, visit www.rspbguernsey.co.uk). Expect to see oystercatchers, shags, cormorants, gulls, egrets, fulmars, razorbills, guillemots, puffins, and many more. The smaller islands are favourites for birdwatchers, particularly the puffins and gannets on Alderney. On Herm there are puffin-watching boat trips and on Sark you can take bird-watching tours with a local fisherman.

CYCLING

Fit cyclists can forget the car on Guernsey and use pedal power to enjoy the scenery. No distance on Guernsey is too far to cycle, though you may find the amount of traffic you encounter off-putting, not to mention the local 4x4s which leave you little space on the narrow country lanes. Outdoor Guernsey (www.outdoorguernsey.co.uk) offer three-hour guided tours, each visiting off-the-beaten-track attractions and starting at different locations.

The most pleasant roads for cycling are the *Ruettes Tranquilles* (Quiet Lanes) where pedestrians, cyclists and horse-riders have priority over cars, and motorists are meant to slow down to a sedate 15mph (24kmh). For information on cycle hire in Guernsey see page 117.

On Sark, where cars are banned, bikes are a popular way of getting around. Unlike Sark, Herm does not allow cycling.

Cyclists taking in the view from Sark across to Brecqhou

GOLF

The number one golf course is the Royal Guernsey Golf Club (www.royalguernsey-golfclub.com), a seaside course by L'Ancresse Bay in the north of the island where visitors need to produce a handicap certificate from a recognised club. But all are welcome at the 18-hole La Grande Mare at Vazon Bay (www.lagrande-mare.com) and the 9-hole par 3 course designed by Tony Jacklin at St Pierre Park Hotel in St Peter Port (www.handpickedhotels.co.uk/stpierrepark).

On Alderney the 9-hole Alderney Golf Club (www.alderneygolfclub.com) is a scenic and testing course, with fine views of France.

HORSE RIDING

The long-established Melrose Farm Riding School (01481-257 267) in Castel caters for all ages and standards.

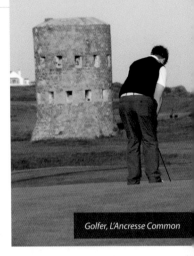
Golfer, L'Ancresse Common

It has an all-weather arena overlooking the west coast and takes rides to Vazon beach.

On Alderney you can explore scenic cliffs and country paths on horseback and, from October to March, beaches too. To book a ride, contact Jill Moore (email: bjmoore65@yahoo.co.uk or text on 07781-421 325).

SHOPPING

Guernsey is not a full member of the EU, and VAT is non-existent. However, this doesn't mean that the shops are packed with bargains. Many of them put up prices for 'freight surcharge'. Moreover, not all goods are VAT-free as some shops retain VAT on goods that have come from the UK. The best buys are wines, spirits and tobacco, and to a lesser extent cosmetics, perfume and jewellery which are all duty-free.

ST PETER PORT

The main shopping centre is St Peter Port, particularly the High Street and its extension, Le Pollet and Lower Pollet where individual, locally-owned shops alternate with the familiar High Street names. Jewellers predominate, selling everything from silver milk cans to gold chain by the yard. Market Square is at its liveliest on Friday mornings in season when stalls are set up with crafts, local produce and ethnic street food.

AROUND THE ISLAND

Jewellery outlets are dotted around the island. **Bruce Russell & Son Gold and Silversmiths** (www.bruce-russell.com) at Le Gron in St Saviours make beautiful items from gold, silver and platinum, including candlesticks, goblets, spoons, caskets and the traditional Guernsey loving cup. The family business has been going strong since 1887 and has the bonus of an 8-acre (3-hectare) award-winning garden and a brasserie and tea room (see page 110). Award-winning jeweller **Catherine Best** (www.catherinebest.com) runs a family business operating from an historic windmill in St Martin and is known for her diverse designs, often styled from rare, fabulously coloured gemstones. Most of the designs are limited editions. At **Guernsey Pearl** (www.guernseypearl.com), opposite Fort Grey on the west coast, the pearls come from the Far East but are made up here. Visitors can watch the pearl stringing and purchase jewellery.

A cluster of attractions in the north of the island are ideal for rainy days. **Oatlands Village** (see page

---

Farmers' Market

The Farmers' Market at Sausmarez Manor on Saturday mornings is well worth a diversion. It has a wonderful range of local produce from Guernsey crabs, beef and cheese to handmade crafts, antiques and plants.

57) provides a convenient one-stop shop for all sorts of hand-made items, from chocolates to perfume bottles. Close by are the **Guernsey Freesia Centre** and **Guernsey Candles** where you can watch wax being dyed and moulded, and children can make their own candle.

Catherine Best necklace

ENTERTAINMENT

Visit the tourist office or pick up a copy of *The Guernsey Press* for details of what's on. Guernsey's premier arts venue is St James's Concert and Assembly Hall (www.stjames.gg), a church in College Street. Guernsey is not the place to go for nightlife, though it does have a few pubs with live music in St Peter Port. The Doghouse (www.doghouse.gg), located on Rohais, is the best venue in town for live entertainment, with live music most nights, plus monthly UK tribute bands. RED (www.red.gg) has a harbour view and a great list of cocktails.

ACTIVITIES FOR CHILDREN

For a traditional family holiday, Guernsey has the ideal ingredients: acres of sandy beaches, crab-filled rock pools, myriad shells to collect and plenty of sporting activities. There's a great castle to explore (Castle Cornet, see page 28) and Sausmarez Manor (see page 38) in St Martin has two adventure play areas and a 9-hole

Guernsey Aquarium

pitch-and-putt golf attraction, while Oatlands Village (see page 57) offers children's rides. On a rainy day you can take youngsters to the Beau Sejour Leisure Centre (www.beausejour.gg) on the hilltop above St Peter Port to enjoy the 25-metre indoor swimming pool and separate children's pool; also tennis and badminton courts and a crèche with activities for older children. Other places worth considering are the Folk and Costume Museum (see page 56), with work sheets and prizes for children, and the Guernsey Museum (see page 34), which has a Discovery Room for youngsters.

There aren't as many attractions on the smaller islands, but youngsters may fall in love with the islands' quaint ways. Because of the considerable walking or cycling involved and because of the inaccessibility of its beaches, Sark can be tough-going for small children. Herm, by contrast, where Shell Beach is just a 10-minute walk from the ferry, is a paradise for any short-legged adventurer.

WHAT'S ON

For full listings go to www.visitguernsey.com/events.

Alderney Literary Festival Mid-Mar. Gathering of historians, biographers and novelists of historical fiction and non-fiction.

Guernsey Heritage Festival May. More than 300 events take place across the islands.

Guernsey Literary Festival End June. Four-day literary event.

Alderney Performing Arts Festival July/Aug. An exciting programme of concerts, shows, dances, street dancing, circus acts and workshops.

Liberation Day 9 May. Islanders celebrate the liberation from the German Occupying forces, which occurred on 9 May 1945.

Alderney Food and Drink Festival: Late June–early July. The island's gastronomic highlight. Food foraging and local delicacies.

Bloomin' Alderney June. Celebrating the islands' flowers and gardens.

Guernsey Street Festival End July–early Aug. Fortnight celebration of talent in all forms of street performers, including music, art and dance.

Sark Sheep Racing July. Sheep, with teddy bears for jockeys, race over a set course.

Lé Viaer Marchi Mid-July. Re-enactment of a 1900s market fair, with traditional music, dance and costume.

Torteval Scarecrow Festival Last weekend in July.

Rocquaine Regatta End July–early Aug. A day of entertainment, activities and fun on Guernsey's west coast.

Alderney Week Early Aug. Week-long carnival and community festival.

Fete d'Etai Mid-Aug. Medieval-themed entertainment at Castle Cornet.

The West Show Mid-Aug. Celebration of agricultural and horticultural traditions on the west coast.

The North Show Late Aug. Family entertainment including the Battle of Flowers with awards for the best floral floats.

Guernsey International Food Festival Mid-Sept Showcasing the best of the island's food through themed diners, guest chefs and more.

Tennerfest Oct–mid-Nov. Restaurants are packed out for six weeks when fixed menus start at £10 at 170 restaurants.

FOOD AND DRINK

Guernsey has a thriving gastronomic scene, particularly in St Peter Port. Eating out is an essential part of life on the island, and with its well-off residents, Guernsey has more than its fair share of up-market restaurants. Even the discerning French come across the Channel to indulge their palates. Annual culinary competitions testify to the islands' gastronomic pride and the islands hold regular food festivals and tasting events. For simpler tastes, there is no shortage of pizzerias, pubs with ploughman's lunches and beach kiosks where you can tuck into a tasty crab sandwich or a Guernsey cream tea.

Seafood is the speciality here and you'd be missing out if your visit didn't include at least one meal that had been harvested from

Fort Grey blue cheese

the sea. The clear, warm waters around the island produce lobsters, prawns, scallops and crabs. Most of the island's small fishing boats return within 24 hours so the bulk of the fish sold is landed on the same day it is caught.

Guernsey crab for sale

Given the proximity to France, it is not surprising that Gallic dishes feature on menus. Firm favourites are *moules marinières, moules-frites,* or *plateau de fruits de mer.* There are good farmhouse cheeses from Normandy and fresh French baguettes can be bought from bakers in St Peter Port (try, for example, Boulangerie Victor Hugo in Le Pollet). There are also plenty of places that cater for British tastes. You never have to go far to find a fry-up for breakfast, fish and chips or roast beef with Yorkshire pudding – the British institution of Sunday lunch is well-preserved.

SEAFOOD

Seafood features on virtually every menu. Your best bet is the fresh catch often chalked up on a blackboard outside restaurants. This will typically include mussels, scallops, shrimps and chancre crabs. Lobster is caught around the Guernsey shores and is served either cold with mayonnaise, Thermidor (braised in brandy or sherry and served in a creamy, mustard-flavoured sauce), or *à la nage,* in a white wine stock. Fish from Guernsey waters include sea bass, bream, brill, sole, grey mullet, monkfish, turbot and mackerel.

Unless you choose a crab sandwich, seafood can be pricey. Fish is sometimes served by weight – ask roughly how much a dish will cost to avoid an unpleasant surprise at the end of the meal.

For a full blow-out, order a Breton-style *plateau de fruits de mer*, and work your way through a king-size banquet of oysters, scallops, crabs, mussels and lobster. The nicely plump chancre crab is the most widely available but the sweeter spider crab is more sought after.

LOCAL PRODUCE

The Channel Islands are famous for their herds of Jersey and Guernsey cows, with their doe eyes and concave faces. Symbolic of

THE GUERNSEY ORMER

If you happen to be on the island between January and April during spring tides, you might spot locals scouring the rocks in search of the near mythical gastropod: the ormer. This indigenous mollusc, related to the abalone, is found beneath rocks on the island's tidal sandbanks, and has a distinctive shell, well camouflaged from the outside but beautifully iridescent inside with a pearly rainbow sheen. Prized for its unique flavour, the ormer was once a staple of island dinner tables. Traditionally the shellfish were carried home in a basket, soaked, shelled, scrubbed, beaten with a steak hammer, browned in a frying pan, then cooked in a casserole with belly of pork, shallots and carrots. Overfishing led to the ormer becoming a gourmet rarity, and nowadays there are regulations to protect the stocks. Ormers can only be fished on specific days – generally those of the full moon, new moon and two days following, between January and April. They must be larger than 8cm (3in) and no breathing equipment, snorkel or diving suit is allowed during collection.

the islands, they feature on numerous souvenirs such as milk jugs and tea towels. The two islands jealously protect the purity of their own distinctive breed of cattle, which means that the milk tastes slightly different. Both breeds produce incomparably rich milk, and in the case of Guernsey's, it is high in beta carotine, giving it the lovely golden colour. Believed to have descended from two breeds of cattle from northern France, the

Guernsey cream tea

Guernsey cow dates back to around 1700, and the purity of the breed has been guaranteed since 1789 when a ban was imposed on the import of live cattle to the islands. Today the Guernsey cows number less than 10,000 globally, and are on the watch list of the American Livestock Breeds Conservancy.

The Guernsey Dairy produces butter the colour of wild buttercups, cheese, ice cream and the renowned thick and golden Guernsey cream, often lavished on scones. It is also liberally spread on the traditional Guernsey *gâche*, a sweet bread made with raisins, sultanas and mixed peel, and pronounced 'gosh'.

Apart from Guernsey cows, the island's best-known export used to be tomatoes. These were introduced in 1865, eventually accounting for 75 percent of Guernsey's income. In more recent times cheaper Dutch imports have usurped 'Guernsey toms' from English shops, forcing the island's horticulturalists to switch their green houses to cut-flower production. Tomatoes are still grown for local consumption, along with celery, courgettes, peppers and most other salad ingredients. Potatoes are grown too, but Guernsey dwellers will bend the knee to the deliciously earthy new potatoes grown by rival Jersey and likely to be found on the menu from March onwards.

The national dish is Guernsey Bean Jar, a variation of the French cassoulet. This hearty dish, comprised of various kinds of dried beans, plus pork, onions and herbs, is traditionally cooked overnight in a stone bean jar and served with crusty bread. There is also a Jersey Bean Jar and the island's emigrants in Canada are reputed to have inspired Mr Heinz's world-famous baked beans.

VRAIC

Vraic (pronounced 'rack' and Guernsey patois for seaweed) was for centuries gathered with horse and cart by St Peter's parishioners to enrich the crops. There are two types of vraic: the weed washed up on the beach after stormy weather and the type cut from the rocks, which was used as fuel by fishermen who could not afford coal or wood. Vraic collection days were party-like, with whole families gathered on the beaches, men wading out to the rocks on foot or going by boat, while women and children collected ormers, crabs and limpets in profusion. Spirits were kept high with vraic buns and cider, and at the end of the day the seaweed was brought up from the bay by horse and cart and families returned home to feast on shellfish. Cutting of vraic from the rocks was only allowed at certain times of year and was closely supervised by parish officials. Vraic days are sometimes held on the beach at L'Eree in celebration of the seaweed, featuring storytellers, foraging walks, cooking demonstrations, traditional stalls and children's activities.

CIDER AND ALE

Cider was first introduced to the Channel Islands by the Normans and until relatively recently it was the main drink on the islands. In the 17th century it was given by farmers to their staff to make up their wages. Today cider aficionados can try the popular Rocquette Cider, made from locally-grown apples. But

Milk o'Punch Sunday

If you happen to be in Alderney on the first Sunday in May, between noon and 2pm, you'll be hailed with a free Milk o'Punch at any of the island's pubs. The punch is made from milk and egg, with a healthy tot of rum and some mystery ingredients.

today the preferred tipple, as in the UK, is a pint of beer. The popularity of imported lager led to a sharp decline in the sales of local breweries. Randalls (www.randallsbrewery.com) established in St Peter Port in 1868, is the only one of the old breweries to survive and today they have a state-of-the-art brewery on St George's Esplanade. Pre-arranged group tours (minimum 12 people) take place on Thursday evenings at 6–7.30pm. Visitors are shown how water, malt hops and yeast are converted into Breda Lager and Patois, Guernsey's only locally-brewed real ale. Another brewery on the island is the Little Big Brew Co, founded in 2020, which produces good quality beers with names like Nigel, Betty and Alan.

Cider and real ale fans head to Herm in June and September for the Ale and Cider festivals, hosted by the Mermaid Tavern. Held over six days, these are lively events with around 30 ales and a dozen ciders to try, and live music on some evenings. For information on dates and booking go to www.herm.com/events.

WHERE TO EAT

You're rarely far from food on any of the islands. Almost every attraction and easily accessible beach has at least a café, there are snug pubs down many country lanes and hotels invariably woo non-residents with bar meals, gourmet menus and cream teas. You can choose from smart seafood restaurants, cosy bistros or seaside cafés, while a smattering of Italian, Portuguese, Chinese and Indian restaurants provide cosmopolitan touches. St Peter Port has by far the best choice and many of its excellent seafood restaurants have fine views of the harbour. The choice of restaurants is clearly more limited on the smaller islands although all three can offer you a slap-up meal.

Eating out at lunchtime, when many restaurants offer good value two-course set menus, is often cheaper than evening dining. Opening times are the same as those in the UK at lunchtime, but evening meals tend to be served earlier, especially at seaside restaurants where last orders are often at 8 or 8.30pm or even earlier. In summer it is usually wise to reserve a table in advance, especially if it's a warm evening and you want to dine alfresco.

Hedge veg stall

CULINARY EVENTS

Late autumn is the time for some real bargains, with dozens of restaurants, including many of the best, offering fixed-price menus from £10. The hugely popular 'Tennerfest' lasts for six weeks from October to mid-November and takes place throughout the Channel Islands. Over 170 eateries offer fixed price menus at heavily slashed prices. It's a great chance to try top quality restaurant meals at a bargain price. Menus are displayed in a special guide in *The Guernsey Press* (the island's daily newspaper) and on the website at www.tennerfest.com.

The island hosts a variety of food events and festivals throughout the year. On certain Sundays from May to

Hedge Veg

As you travel around the island you'll see unmanned stalls selling home-grown fruit and veg, known locally as 'hedge veg'. You choose what you want – from cut flowers and new potatoes to courgettes and asparagus – then leave the correct change in an honesty box.

September, St Peter Port seafront is closed to traffic and transformed by market stalls and alfresco dining. Visitors can take part in cookery demonstrations and free tasting of traditional dishes. During the International Food Festival in September world cuisine is showcased by guest chefs and on restaurant menus, while local produce takes centre stage. The festival hosts a variety of events such as foraging workshops, cocktail masterclasses and beach-based cook offs with competing local chefs. At the end of June virtually all of Alderney's restaurants take part in the Alderney Food and Drink Festival.

Country and farmers' markets throughout the island sell local produce. Among the best is the Saturday morning Farmers' market at Sausmarez Manor (see page 38) with a wide range of locally-made products, fresh fruit and vegetables and plants. The market also sells antiques and bric-à-brac,. You can experience Guernsey both on foot and with food on the Tasty Walks (see page 90). For up-to-date information on events, go to www.visitguernsey.com.

WHERE TO EAT

We have used the following symbols to give an idea of the price for a two-course meal with a glass of wine, excluding service charge.

££££	**over £40**
£££	**£30–40**
££	**£25–30**
£	**under £25**

ST PETER PORT

The Brasserie Restaurant ££££ *St Ann's Place, tel: 01481-724 921,* www.theoghotel.com/dining-and-drinks/the-brasserie-restaurant. Overlooking the hotel's garden, this bright and airy conservatory celebrates local, organic ingredients. In the evening dinner is accompanied by live piano music. Daily 12-2pm & 6–9.30pm.

Fat Rascals £££ *2 Lefebvre Street, tel: 01481-728 515,* www.fatrascal.gg. This laid-back, welcoming spot serves up creative brunches including pulled pork rosti, "Rascal Rancheros" and Turkish eggs. In the evening expect hearty mains and delicious cocktails. The bar is open until midnight on Fridays and Saturdays. Mon–Sat 10am–2pm & 6pm–9pm, Sun 9am–2pm.

La Frégate ££££ *Les Cotils, tel: 01481-724 624,* www.lafregatehotel.com. Outstanding, quite formal hotel restaurant with magical views of the harbour and outer islands. The emphasis is on Guernsey seafood and fish, cooked with precision and artfully presented. The restaurant prides itself on its wines, 'which should enthral and excite the connoisseur but not bamboozle the enthusiast'. Regarded by many as the best seafood restaurant on the island. Wed–Sat lunch & dinner, Sun lunch.

The Hook £££ *North Plantation, tel: 01481-701 373,* www.thehook.gg. Come for steak, seafood or sushi at this waterfront restaurant. If you fancy pushing the boat out, try half a Guernsey lobster in lime and chilli butter. Tue–Sat 12–2.30pm & 6–10pm.

Leopard Bar & Restaurant ££££ *Cambridge Park, tel: 01481-726 221*, www.dukeofrichmond.com/dining-and-drinks/leopard-bar-and-restaurant. Award-winning restaurant serving up the freshest Guernsey seafood on the terrace or in the airy conservatory. In the evening you can enjoy drinks in the glitzy leopard-print decorated bar. Daily lunch & dinner.

Mora £££ *The Quay, tel: 01481-715 053*, www.mora.gg. Spread over two floors, Mora offers fine views over the harbour. The busy ground-floor brasserie, serving tapas, gourmet burgers and shared platters, doubles as a cocktail bar. The more peaceful restaurant upstairs showcases the best of Guernsey's seafood with abundant seafood platters and Guernsey lobster. Tues–Sun lunch & dinner.

Le Nautique £££ *Quay Steps, tel: 01481-721 714;* www.lenautiquerestaurant.co.uk. One of Guernsey's top seafood restaurants, with lovely views over the marina if you're lucky enough to secure a window seat. Chef and owner Günter Botzenhart gives classical dishes a modern twist and his menu is constantly changing to make the most of produce in season. Mon–Fri 12–2pm & 7–10pm, Sat 6.30–10pm.

Da Nello's ££££ *46 Le Pollett, tel: 01481-721 552*, www.danello.gg. An Italian favoured by locals, with an attractive covered courtyard. Expect a warm welcome and a wide range of traditional pasta, seafood and meat dishes. Tues–Sat 12–2pm & 6–9.30pm, Sun 12–2pm.

Octopus ££££ *Havelet Bay, tel: 01481-722400*, www.octopusgsy.co.uk. Superb seafront dining serving fantastic local seafood. Specialities include oven-grilled oysters with seaweed and Champagne sabayon, whole Chancre crab with chili butter and the hot seafood pot special cooked in a charcoal and clay oven. Also includes an inventive take on the vegetarian option: choose three of your favourite ingredients and let the chef create you a unique dish. Thu–Mon lunch and dinner.

Old Quarter Restaurant ££ *15 Mansell Street, tel: 01481-727 268*, www.old-quarter.co.uk. Set among cobbled streets, a warm welcome awaits you at this restaurant serving honest, no nonsense food with a slight Irish slant, in honour of the owner's roots. Mon–Sat lunch and dinner, closed Mon lunch.

Le Petit Bistro ££ *56 Lower Pollet, tel: 01481-725 055,* www.petitbistro.co.uk. Authentic French cuisine in atmospheric bistro. Specialities feature *coq au vin*, *coquilles St Jacques* and frogs' legs. Excellent-value set lunches and early-bird dinners. The adjoining Le Petit Café serves lighter bites. Tue–Sat lunch and dinner.

La Piazza ££ *Trinity Square, tel: 01481-725 085.* This buzzing Italian offers some excellent-value meal deals, friendly attentive staff and seats outside in summer. Expect great seafood alongside the traditional pasta and pizza. Mon–Sat lunch and dinner.

Pier 17 £££ *Albert Pier, tel: 01481-720 823,* www.pier17restaurant.com. One of the island's most popular restaurants with a stylish contemporary setting and great views over the working harbour and Castle Cornet. Book well in advance. Tue–Sat lunch and dinner.

The Swan Inn £ *St Julian's Avenue, tel: 01481-728969.* This welcoming Victorian corner pub is a favourite for evening drinks and gastropub fare. Come for hearty helpings of home-made pies and burgers or the chef's weekly-changing dishes, such as house-smoked rack of lamb or line-caught Guernsey seabass with tapenade, garlic and almond cream. Meals are served both in the traditional downstairs bar or the stylish first-floor dining room. Closed Sun and Mon.

Terrace Café Bar & Balcony ££ *St Pierre Park Hotel, tel: 01481-728 282,* www.handpickedhotels.co.uk/stpierrepark. The chef is a keen advocate of fresh Guernsey produce and fuss-free techniques, so expect dishes such as Guernsey white crab and chancre crab in spicy kombu stock, lemongrass and lime. Dine in modern stylish surroundings or on a large terrace overlooking a lake. Daily.

AROUND THE ISLAND

Fermain Bay

Fermain Beach Café ££ *tel: 01481-238 636,* www.fermainbeachcafe.gg. This seafood café-cum-bistro is a great place to refuel after a bracing walk along the coast. Choose from Guernsey crab sandwiches, salmon ciabatta or mouth-watering cakes and enjoy the views of this lovely bay. The secluded location entails a fairly steep walk down the hill – but it is well worth it. You need to book well in advance for evening meals (high season only). Daily 10am–6pm (later in high season), Oct–Mar weekends only.

St Martin's

La Barbarie Hotel £££ *Saint's Road, St Martin, tel: 01481-235 217,* www.la-barbariehotel.com. This charming rural hotel is known for its cuisine. Come for creamy crab bisque, grilled fillet of brill or slow-cooked short rib of beef. Great dessert options include Calvados mousse with apple cider sorbet and toffee sauce, baked vanilla cheesecake and a selection of Guernsey-based Le Hechet Farm ice cream. Daily.

Bella Luce Hotel £££ *La Fosse, St Martin's, tel: 01481-238 764,* www.bellalucehotel.com. This is a stylish hotel in the peaceful green lanes of St Martin's, where you can come for light bar meals, a leisurely afternoon tea or gourmet Modern European cuisine. The head chef is passionate about local produce, and uses local fishermen and artisanal foodmakers. Bella's bistro opens out onto a lovely walled garden for summer meals. Wed–Sat lunch and dinner, Sun lunch.

Moulin Huet Tea Rooms £ *Rue de Huet Moulin Huet, St Martin's, tel: 07781 464825.* This hidden gem is worth seeking out with its spectacular views of the bay and a great selection of homemade cakes and cream teas along with light lunches. Daily 10am–4.30pm (till 6pm at peak times), closed Oct–Mar.

Forest

Le Gouffre ££ *Le Gouffre, tel: 01481-264121.* This café/restaurant is the perfect spot for cliff-top walkers in need of respite: peaceful, with sunny terrace, (partial) sea views and excellent, freshly-prepared fare. Expect Mediterranean fish soup, salt and pepper squid, steaks and light lunches. The bar is a perfect spot to watch the sun go down over a glass of wine. Closed Mon, and Tue and Sun dinner.

St Saviour

Auberge du Val ££ *Sous L'Église, St Saviours, tel: 01481-263 862*. Very popular traditional *auberge* in an attractive rural setting. Ideal for a simple bistro-style lunch or more adventurous evening meals using ingredients fresh from their garden. Opening times erratic, call ahead.

The Farmhouse £££ *St Saviours, tel: 01481-264 181, www.thefarmhouse.gg.* In a hotel converted from an old farmhouse, the restaurant and bright, airy courtyard have a contemporary look and modern cuisine. Light lunches can be enjoyed by the outdoor pool in summer. Also offers a picnic menu featuring ham hock terrine and smoked salmon, alongside home-made cakes. Everything is bundled up in a rented hamper to accompany you on your picnic. Daily.

Patois Brasserie ££ *Le Gron, St Saviours (in the gardens of the Bruce Russell & Son Goldsmiths complex), tel: 01481-263 222, www.patoisbrasserie.gg.* This farmhouse-style brasserie-cum-tearoom has won favour with its fair prices, home-made cakes and desserts, and hot lunches. The restaurant promotes locally-sourced seasonal ingredients where possible, and makes its own bean jar (see page 102). Daily 9am–4pm.

Torteval

Imperial Hotel Restaurant ££ *Rocquaine Bay, Torteval, tel: 01481-264 044, www.theimperial.gg.* Sea views towards Fort Grey are the big attraction here. You can come any time for bar or main meals from the modern British menu or coffee in the gardens. The à la carte menu features seafood straight from the bay as well as lots of great vegan and vegetarian options. Lunch and dinner, closed Mon & Tue in Nov.

L'Erée

Taste of India £ *Sunset Cottage, L'Erée, tel: 01481-264 516,* www.tasteofindiaci.com. Stroll across the beach then stoke up at this very popular Indian restaurant, just across from the bay, and enjoy the sunset. Takeaways are available. Daily.

Cobo Bay

Cobo Bay Hotel Restaurant £££ *Cobo Bay Hotel, Cobo Bay, tel: 01481-257 102,* www.cobobayhotel.com. Spectacular sea views and sunsets are a big attraction here. The menu changes with the seasons, but you could start with diver-caught scallops and follow with monk fish or rib-eye steak. The restaurant has won awards for the quality of food and service. Lunch and dinner daily, closed for lunch in winter.

Cobo Fish and Chip Bar £ *Cobo Coast Road, tel: 01481-254 276.* Buy fish and chips from this basic but popular chippie and enjoy them while watching the glorious sunset over Cobo Bay across the road. Mon–Sat 11.30am–2pm and 4.30–9.30pm, Sun from 4pm (later in high season).

Cobo Tearoom £ *Cobo Coast Road, tel: 01481-253 366, Tues–Fri 10am–4pm, Sat–Sun 9am–5pm.* Traditional family-run tearoom overlooking Cobo Bay serving homemade cakes, traditional lunches and breakfast on the weekend. Sit out on the terrace on a sunny day or grab a cosy window seat and enjoy the view.

The Rockmount ££ *Cobo Coast Road, tel: 01481-252 778,* www.therocky. gg. Family-friendly gastro pub with fabulous bay views and catering for all tastes. Along with pub favourites you'll find twice-baked goats cheese soufflé, Guernsey Cheddar gnocchi, *moules marinière* or Guernsey crab salad. Great dessert menu too, featuring the "Rockmount Mess" (stewed rhubarb, meringue and Guernsey double cream) and an Oreo chocolate cheesecake with coconut sorbet. Mon–Sat lunch and dinner, Sun lunch only.

Castel

Crabby Jack's Restaurant *Vazon Bay, tel: 01481-257489,* www.thechristies-group.gg/crabby-jacks. Fun, friendly restaurant with an outdoor children's play area lined with tables so parents can relax and enjoy a meal whilst the kids play. The menu is casual and there's something for everyone including hot dogs, pizza and plenty of vegetarian options. It goes without saying that there is a great kid's menu. Tue–Sun lunch and dinner.

Fleur du Jardin ££ *Kings Mill, Castel, tel: 01481-257 996,* www.fleurdujardin. com. This country hotel serves some of the best gastro-pub fare in the Channel Islands. The emphasis is on local produce: superb locally-bred beef, line-caught seabass, west coast scallops or a locally-sourced crab sandwich. The desserts are worth a try too, featuring homemade passion fruit sorbet and local Guernsey ice cream. Lunch and dinner, closed Tue.

Vale

The Beach House £ *Pembroke Bay, Vale, tel: 01481-246 494,* www.beach-houseguernsey.com. Right on the beach in a stark modern building, with a viewing gallery for meals above. Open for breakfast through to dinner, serving sandwiches, burgers and Pembroke fish and chips. July–mid-Sept daily 9am–8pm, off-season Tue–Fri 11am–8pm, Sat–Sun 9am–8pm.

Roc Salt ££ *Mont Cuet Road, Chouet, Vale, tel: 01481-246 129,* www.rocsalt. gg. This is one of the best fish restaurants in the north of the island. Menus change regularly and dishes are simply cooked and flavoursome. Décor is shabby chic, and the balcony has fine views over Chouet Bay. Tue–Sat lunch and dinner, Sun lunch, closed Jan.

Surfside at Port Soif £ *Port Soif, Vale, tel: 01481-253 709.* Excellent value home-made food including bacon butties, fresh crab sandwiches and generously-buttered Guernsey *gâche* (fruit loaf). The outdoor seating overlooks the bay. Early Apr–Oct daily 9.30am–6pm.

Herm

Conservatory Restaurant £££ *White House Hotel, Herm Harbour, tel: 01481-750 075,* www.herm.com. Traditional hotel restaurant where you can enjoy Guernsey seafood and lamb or full afternoon tea with uninterrupted sea views. Meals served on the lawn in fine weather. Extensive wine list, with many bought directly from Bordeaux Châteaux. Usually daily for afternoon tea and dinner end Apr–Oct.

Mermaid Tavern ££ *Herm Harbour, tel: 01481-750 050;* www.herm.com. The social hub of the island, with pub lunches and a good choice of beers and wines. Steaks, fish and vegetarian dishes can be eaten out in the courtyard or inside the charming pub. The Mermaid is the venue of the occasional real ale and cider festivals. Apr–Sept lunch and dinner daily, restricted hours off-season.

The Ship Inn Brasserie ££ *White House Hotel, Herm Harbour, tel: 01481-750 075; www.herm.com.* Serving excellent cuisine from the kitchens of The White House Hotel, the Ship Inn has a more informal atmosphere than the Conservatory Restaurant. Come for a fry-up breakfast, seafood or sandwich lunches, cake and cream teas or full dinners with good-value wines. Meals can be taken alfresco on the patio, in the bar by the log fire or in the restaurant. Apr–end Sep daily from 9am, restricted hours off-season.

Sark

La Sablonnerie ££££ *Little Sark, tel: 01481-832 061, www.sablonneriesark. com.* Located on peaceful Little Sark this is the perfect place to stop on a walking or cycling tour. You can enjoy snacks, cream teas and seafood platters in the flower-filled tea gardens or a lunch based on the ingredients produced on the hotel's organic farm. For guests at this charming old farmhouse, or others staying in Sark, there are candlelit dinners. Lunch and dinner mid-Apr–late Oct.

Stocks ££££ *tel: 01481-832 001, www.stockshotel.com.* Fine dining in elegant surrounds. Choose from à la carte or bistro menus and make the most of the fruits of Sark's seas: mackerel, seabass, turbot and hand-dived scallops. In season, lobsters are caught within a three-mile radius of the hotel and normally require 24 hours' notice. Daily.

Alderney

Braye Beach Hotel £££ *Braye Street, tel: 01481-824 300, www.brayebeach. com.* For lunch, book a table at The Brasserie overlooking the lovely Braye beach and tuck into crab cakes or local lobster salad. For dinner, The Vaults (situated in the hotel's converted wine vault) offers more contemporary surroundings and serves up steaks, classic sides and cocktails. Wed–Sun lunch and dinner.

Braye Chippie £ *Braye Harbour, tel: 01481-823 475*. Very popular chippie, with plenty of seating inside and out, right by the harbour. Bring your own bottle. Wed–Sat 5–8pm, also Tue & Sun in high season.

Bumps Bar & Bistro ££ *Victoria Street, St Anne, tel: 01481-823 197*. A long-standing favourite among islanders for superb seafood, along with steaks and vegetarian options. The chef is also the owner, which is always good news. Service is attentive and friendly, and there's a sunny patio for alfresco dining. Wed–Sun lunch and dinner, except Sun dinner off-season.

Cantina Number 6 ££ *6 Braye Street, tel: 01481-824 063*. Come to this buzzing bistro-type place for a really pleasant variation on the normal pub/restaurant setting. The menu mostly consists of tasty tapas plates, both large and small. A specials board adds to the already extensive and varied choice. Tue–Sat lunch and dinner.

Georgian House ££ *Victoria Street, St Anne, tel: 01481-822 471*, www.georgi-analderney.com. This family-run hotel restaurant has a lovely sheltered garden at the rear. The menu is a mix of traditional English pub and European cuisine, with emphasis on seafood, and use of local and sustainable produce where possible. Very friendly staff. Lunch and dinner, lunch only Sun.

Jack's Brasserie £ *Victoria Street, St Anne, tel: 01481-823 933*, www.jacksalder-ney.com. This is a popular spot for breakfasts, light lunches, and coffee and cakes. With a sunny terrace on the High Street, it's a good spot to relax and watch the world go by. For dinner expect an Italian twist: arancini to start and saffron carbonara, slow-braised oxtail ragu and tiger prawn risotto for mains. Mon, Tue, Fri & Sat 9am–8pm, Wed & Thu 9am–3pm with extended hours in high season.

Le Pesked ££ *Newtown Road, Braye, tel: 01481-823 841*, www.lepeskedhar-bourlights.com. Distinctly French flavours are delivered with skill at this delightful restaurant set in the cobbled streets off St Annes. Run by Brittany chef David Ollivrin, his classic French cooking is given a modern twist and will not disappoint. The dessert menu is good (and extensive) and features specialities such as *crêpes suzette*, chocolate *marquise* and baked meringue with caramel *crème anglaise*. Book ahead. Daily.

TRAVEL ESSENTIALS

PRACTICAL INFORMATION

A

ACCOMMODATION

From simple B&Bs to stylishly converted farmhouses and chic boutique hotels, Guernsey offers accommodation to cater for most tastes. But while places to stay are plentiful you won't find many bargains. The best deals tend to be packages that include air or sea transport. Many of the hotels offer this option on their websites; alternatively you can do it through specialist operators. For example, Channel Islands Direct (www.channelislandsdirect.co.uk) or FlyGuernsey (www.flyguernsey.com) offer deals whereby the total cost for a week's holiday in a hotel, travel included (and sometimes car hire), is less than the cost of accommodation alone booked through the hotel. Rates are almost invariably cheaper off-season and there are some great deals at the hotels that remain open in winter. For rooms in July and August book well ahead. Supplements are usually charged for sea view rooms, although it's often worth the extra for the fabulous view you wake up to.

Old-fashioned values are still often adhered to, but that doesn't mean you won't get Wi-fi or power showers in the upper bracket hotels. Guernsey has one five-star hotel, the Old Government House Hotel & Spa (see page 136), and some of the four-star hotels have undergone stylish revamps.

Self-catering is increasingly popular, whether in seaside apartments or country cottages. For utter isolation Fort Clonque (see page 141) on Alderney sleeps up to 13 and can be rented from the Landmark Trust.

For details of accommodation on all the islands visit the relevant tourist office website (see page 130).

As a base, St Peter Port offers the best sightseeing, shopping and dining options. Buses from here will take you all over the island; it is also convenient for hopping across to Herm or Sark. But wherever you stay on the island you are never far from the capital.

AIRPORTS

Guernsey Airport (tel: 01481-227 766; www.airport.gg) is located in the parish of Forest, 3 miles (5km) southwest of St Peter Port. Arrival at the small airport is normally stress-free with quick luggage pick-up, customs and passport control, and a taxi rank and bus stop right outside. The airport is on several regular bus routes including nos. 71/92/93/95, which all take you to the St Peter Port bus terminus. Tickets can be bought on the bus (contactless payment only). A taxi from the airport to St Peter Port costs from around £16–18 depending on the location of your hotel. Rental cars can be picked up at the airport.

Tiny Alderney Airport is just over a mile from St Anne. Aurigny (www.aurignynew.com) is the main airline for the island. Taxis meet arriving planes and rental cars can be booked.

B

BICYCLE RENTAL

Guernsey's hills are quite surmountable for any cyclist who is reasonably fit, but if you haven't biked for 20 years it's probably not the place to restart. You can feel very surrounded by cars at times and it can be a tight squeeze passing larger vehicles on tiny lanes. The most peaceful roads are the Ruettes Tranquilles (Quiet Lanes) which together form a network across the parishes of Castel, Forest, St Andrew, St Martin, St Sampson, St Savour and the Vale. These signposted lanes have a speed limit of 15mph (24kmh), though not all motorists adhere to the limit. There are coastal paths suitable for cyclists along the west coast and a 2-mile (3km) cycle path on the sea side of St Peter Port with great views of cruise ships and neighbouring islands. Cycling is not permitted on nature trails or along the cliff paths in the south of the island. Guernsey Tourist Information provide 11 island routes with maps, ranging from 7 to 12 miles (11 to 19km), which can be downloaded from their website.

On car-free **Sark** pedal power is the preferred means of transport and you should keep to the left despite the absence of cars. You can't miss the bike-hire shops on Mermaid Lane and along The Avenue. In high season book in advance. On **Alderney** the size of the island and its peaceful lanes make it ideal for cycling. Cycles can be hired in Victoria Street, St Anne. Visitors are forbidden to cycle on **Herm**.

Those travelling to Guernsey on Condor Ferries can bring bikes to the island free of charge.

Bikes can be hired from:

GUERNSEY

Adventure Cycles, Grande Rue, St Martins (tel: 01481-232 855). Bikes for hire, plus guided bike tours are offered through their partners Outdoor Guernsey (www.outdoorguernsey.gg) visiting sights of historical and natural interest.

Millard & Co, 9–11 Victoria Street, St Peter Port (tel: 01481-720 777; www.millards.org).

Go Guernsey Cycle Hire, North Plantation, St Peter Port (tel: 07781-103 692; www.go-guernsey.gg).

SARK

A and B Cycles, Mermaid Lane (tel: 01481-832 844; www.atobcycles.com**).**

Avenue Cycle Hire, The Avenue (tel: 01481-832 102; www.avenuecyclessark.co.uk).

ALDERNEY

Cycle and Surf, St Anne (tel: 01481-822 286 or 07781-154 045; www.cycleandsurf.co.uk). Electric bikes available.

BUDGETING FOR YOUR TRIP

Costs of flights from the UK to Guernsey vary hugely from around £80 to £400 return, depending on the airline, time of year and day of the week (weekends are usually more expensive). Return flights from London Gatwick or Southampton to Guernsey with Aurigny cost from around £120 per person. In high season the Condor ferry from Poole to Guernsey costs £300–500 return for a family of four with a car. A three-star hotel charges £100–200 for a double room, a luxury hotel £200–300. Restaurant and bar prices are similar or slightly higher than those in the UK. Most attractions are free for young children. Museum admissions for adults range from £4 to £10. A taxi from the airport to St Peter Port costs £16–18.

C

CAMPING

Guernsey has some attractive and peaceful campsites: the centrally located Fauxquets Valley Farm Camping Site (www.fauxquets.co.uk) was AA Campsite of the Year 2015 for South West England; La Bailloterie Camping (www.camp-inginguernsey.com) is in a rural setting in the north and Vaugrat Camping (www.vaugratcampsite.com) is just a short walk from the northwest beaches. Alderney's Saye Bay site (www.sayebeachcamping.co.uk) lies directly behind the north coast's sandy bays. Of Sark's two basic sites, La Valette (www.sercq.com) is dramatically located near the cliffs. The island of Herm has a simple, well-run campsite (www.herm-island.com/camping). Glamping experiences are available on Guernsey and Sark.

CAR HIRE

Car hire prices are similar to those in the UK, fuel is slightly cheaper. A valid driving licence is required with no endorsements for dangerous or drunken driving in the last five years. Drivers must have held a full licence for a year and must be over 20 or 21 (sometimes 25) years of age, depending on the company. There are also varying maximum age restrictions. Car hire companies in Guernsey are plentiful and there is little difference in price between the international and local companies. Expect to pay around £160 for a week's rental of a small car, with an extra £5 a day if you hire a satnav. All rented cars are branded with a large letter H on the number plate.

GUERNSEY

Europcar (tel: 01481-239 511; www.europcarguernsey.com)

Hertz (tel: 0800 735 1014; www.hertzci.com)

Value Rent a Car (agents for Avis; tel: 01481-243 547; www.valuerentacar.co.uk).

Rhino Car Hire (tel: 0345-508 9845; www.rhinocarhire.com).

ALDERNEY

Braye Hire Cars (tel: 01481-823 881; www.brayehirecars.com).

CLIMATE

The Channel Islands have the highest average number of sunshine hours in the British Isles, although the summer temperatures are no higher than those in some parts of southern England. As in the UK, the best months to go are from May to September, the hottest months being July and August. High temperatures in mid-summer are tempered by sea breezes.

The sea temperatures are refreshing for swimming, averaging 62.8°F (17.1°C) in summer. The Channel Islands have one of the largest tidal movements in the world.

The following chart gives the average maximum temperature for St Peter Port, Guernsey:

	J	F	M	A	M	J	J	A	S	O	N	D
°C	8	9	10	11	14	17	19	20	18	15	11	10
°F	47	49	50	52	58	62	67	67	64	59	52	49

CLOTHING

The climate is similar to that of the southern part of the UK so take a couple of sweaters and a rainproof jacket even in mid-summer. Otherwise T-shirts and shorts/skirts should suffice, not forgetting a sunhat, sunglasses and sun cream – the sun's rays can be deceptively strong. One of the best ways of seeing the islands is on foot so a stout pair of shoes is useful. Topless bathing is generally accepted, though far from widespread, and baring all on the island is inappropriate. Shopping in a swimsuit in St Peter Port is best avoided, too. Some nightclubs ban jeans and trainers.

CRIME AND SAFETY

Guernsey is a safe place for a holiday but it is worth taking all the usual precautions: always lock car doors and don't leave your valuables unattended. Dial 999 for police, fire, ambulance or coastal rescue services. Report a loss or theft to the police within 24 hours if an insurance claim is to be made.

D

DRIVING

Many roads are very narrow, with high hedges or granite walls and visibility can be poor. The lanes are used by tractors, cyclists, pedestrians, as well as buses and cars, so be aware of your surroundings. Signposting is poor, some satnavs don't work and it is easy to lose your way, although on such a small island it's unlikely you will be lost for long.

Given the narrow lanes and the maximum speed limit of 35mph (55kmh) (and a good deal less in towns and along the Ruettes Tranquilles or Quiet Lanes that have a limit of 15mph/24kmh) there is no point in bringing or hiring a turbo-charged car. A limited number of touring caravans and motorhomes can be accommodated on the authorised camp sites on the island but must comply with certain conditions. A caravan/motorhome permit, which should be obtained in advance from the campsite, must be available for inspection by the ferry operator and the Guernsey Border Agency.

Rules of the Road The rules reflect those of the UK: driving is on the left, seat belts are compulsory for adult front seat passengers, children must wear belts or a suitable child/infant restraint in both front and rear seats; it is an offence to hold a mobile phone whilst driving. Fixed alcohol limits and roadside breath testing are similar to the UK. Police can and do make random checks and penalties are severe.

A wide yellow line across the junction of a minor road means stop and give way to traffic on the major road. A yellow arrow on the road warns of a junction ahead; a single yellow line along the roadside means that vehicles cannot park or wait at any time. Many junctions on Guernsey have a filter-in-turn system, marked by a cross-hatched yellow box painted on the road. You must not enter the box until your exit is clear.

Parking Most on-street parking and car parks in main shopping areas require a parking clock to indicate your time of arrival. Some rental companies leave the clock in the car, if not ask them to supply one. Alternatively they can be purchased from the Driving & Vehicle Licensing Office (Bulwer Avenue), Guernsey Information Centre, garages and from some newsagents. Although you have to pay for the card (£3) the actual parking is free. If you have just arrived and have a GB number plate, a note in the window of the time you arrive at the car park will suffice.

Most of the parking near the centre of St Peter Port is short stay (two or three hours). The major town car parks are on the Harbour piers, the largest being the North Beach area where two- and three- hour parking is nearly always available. There is no park-and-ride service, but if you are going to be in town for longer than three hours, or if you are going on a day trip to one of the neighbouring islands, there are several convenient 10-hour car parks. A bit further out, there are various options (up to 23-hour), although these do fill up early.

E

ELECTRICITY

The current is the same as that of the UK, 240 volts AC, with British-style three-pin sockets. Visitors from other European countries will need an adapter; those from the US will also need a transformer.

EMBASSIES AND HIGH COMMISSIONS

Australia Australian High Commission, Australia House, The Strand, London WC2B 4LA; tel: 020-7379 4334; www.uk.embassy.gov.au.

Canada Canada High Commission, Canada House, Trafalgar Square, London SW1Y 5BJ; tel: 020-7004 6000; www.canadainternational.gc.ca.

New Zealand New Zealand High Commission, 1 Pall Mall East, London SW1Y 5AU; tel: 020-7930 8422; www.mfat.govt.nz.

Republic of Ireland Irish Embassy, 17 Grosvenor Place, London SW1X 7HR; tel: 020-7235 2171; www.embassyofireland.co.uk.

South Africa South Africa High Commission, South Africa House, Trafalgar Square, London WC2N 5DP; tel: 020-7451 7299; www.southafricahouse.uk.

United States US Embassy, 33 Nine Elms Lane, London SW11 7US; tel: 020-7499 9000; www.usembassy.gov.

EMERGENCIES

Dial 999 for police, fire, ambulance or coastal rescue services. The Princess Elizabeth Hospital, at Rue Mignot, St Andrews, GY6 8TW (tel: 01481-725 241) has a 24-hour emergency unit. There is no reciprocal health agreement between Guernsey and the UK and hospital treatment is charged for, with a very limited number of exemptions. Primary Comprehensive medical insurance is therefore strongly recommended.

Herm has no medical facilities, though helicopter-borne emergency services are available. The Sark Medical Practice (tel: 01481-832 045; www. sarkmedical.co.uk) has a drop-in surgery Mon–Sat 8.30–1.30pm, a booked surgery from 8.30–1pm (except Wed, Sat & Sun) and an out-of-hours emergency service. For serious cases patients can be transferred, usually by the St John Ambulance boat, to the Princess Elizabeth Hospital in Guernsey. Alderney has the small Mignot Memorial Hospital (tel: 01481-822 822) and The Island Medical Centre at Le Val (tel: 01481-822 077; imc-alderney.com).

Road accidents involving personal injury or serious damage must be reported to the police within 24 hours. Minor accidents not involving injury need not be reported provided the names and addresses of those concerned are exchanged. If in doubt contact the island police on 01481-222 222.

G

GETTING THERE

Year-round air and sea packages, short breaks, flights and accommodation can all be arranged through specialist tour operators. For details see www.visitguernsey.com.

From the UK

By air. All visitors flying to the Channel Islands need a passport or photo ID. Regular year-round flights operate from airports throughout the UK (but not Heathrow), with added services in high season. Flights take 40 minutes from London Gatwick and as little as 30 minutes from some regional airports. **British Airways** (www.britishairways.com) flies direct to Guernsey from London City between June and September. **Aurigny** (tel: 01481-267 267; www.aurigny.com) flies to Guernsey from Gatwick, Manchester, East Midlands, Leeds

Bradford, Bristol, Exeter, Norwich and Southampton. Loganair (www.loganair. co.uk) flies to Guernsey from Southampton. Although the low-cost airlines have brought down the prices of getting to Guernsey the airport charges are high and real bargains are hard to come by. The cheapest fares are normally secured by booking well in advance on the internet and avoiding weekends and the busiest times of year. Aurigny provide an island-hopping service between Jersey, Alderney and Guernsey.

From the US, Canada, Australia, New Zealand and South Africa, the most efficient route is via London Gatwick, from which frequent daily flights serve Guernsey.

By sea. The only ferry line from the UK to Guernsey is **Condor Ferries** (tel: 0345-609 1026; www.condorferries.com) who operate services all year round. The state-of-the-art trimaran, 'Liberation', accommodating up to 880 passengers and 245 cars, departs from Poole and takes three hours to Guernsey. It is not uncommon for boats to be cancelled or delayed because of the weather conditions, particularly off-season. Facilities include a cafeteria, several bars, a soft play area for children and a duty-free shop with some excellent deals, especially on alcohol. Club-class seating is available, with reclining seats and, for an extra charge, steward service.

Condor Ferries also operate a slower service from Portsmouth on the conventional Clipper car/passenger ferry. The return crossing is overnight with the option of one-, two-, three- or four-berth cabins and en suite facilities. Fast ferry services to Guernsey from Jersey and St Malo in France are also operated by Condor Ferries.

From Guernsey, it is a 20-minute ferry hop to Herm and 50 minutes to Sark; Jersey and Alderney are each a 20-minute flight away; Jersey is one hour by sea, Alderney 1 hour and 25 minutes.

Visitors bringing their own car must have an insurance certificate, the complete vehicle registration document and a valid driving licence or International Driving Permit. Bikes can be taken across on Condor ferries free of charge.

Package holidays. The islands' tourist information offices provide details of UK tour operators with Channel Islands programmes. Tour companies specialising in Guernsey include Premier Holidays (tel: 0844-493 7531, www.premier-holidays.co.uk/guernsey), Channel Islands Direct (tel: 0800-640 9058, www.channelislandsdirect.co.uk) and Guernsey Travel (tel: 01534-496 660 , www.guernseytravel.com).

Overseas visitors should contact the British Tourist Authority in their own country (www.visitbritain.com).

GUIDES AND TOURS

Island Coachways (tel: 01481-720 210; www.icw.gg) offer twice-weekly guided coach tours around the island in summer and also offer Heritage and Occupation tours. Island Taxis (tel: 01481-700 500; www.islandtaxis.gg) offer individual coastal tours that allow you to stop and take photographs.

Walking tours. Guernsey has around 20 accredited guides offering walks to suit all abilities and interests. These include walks to wild and windswept Lihou Island, hidden green lanes, Victor Hugo's House, guided photo tours taking in the most scenic viewpoints of Guernsey, and walking tours of Herm and Alderney. For full details go to www.guernseyguidedtours.com or visit the Guernsey Information Centre in St Peter Port.

H

HEALTH AND MEDICAL CARE

There is no reciprocal health agreement between Guernsey and the UK and apart from treatment solely within Guernsey's A&E department visitors have to pay for medical services and treatment. This includes emergency hospital treatments (such as operations) not within A&E, repatriation and out-patient appointments. Doctors and dentists are in private practice and all patients are required to pay for treatment and prescriptions. UK visitors are therefore advised to take out comprehensive health insurance or check that their existing policy covers travel to the island. Australia and New Zealand have reciprocal care agreements with Guernsey which cover emergency hospital treatment.

The Princess Elizabeth Hospital, (Rue Mignot, St Andrews, GY6 8TW; tel:

01481-725 241) has a 24-hour emergency unit. The majority of GP surgeries provide a service for visitors. The Guernsey Information Centre can provide details of island surgeries, alternatively a list of doctors is available at post offices, or ask your hotel. Medical prescriptions can be dispensed at any of the island pharmacies. Boots has an outlet on the High Street in St Peter Port and provides a full range of over-the-counter and prescription medicines.

See www.visitguernsey.gg for the latest Covid-19 vaccination protocol.

L

LANGUAGE

English is spoken throughout all the Channel Islands. Some older citizens may communicate in Jèrriais, Guernésiais and Sercquiais – the local patois based on Norman French – in Jersey, Guernsey and Sark respectively, but you're more likely to come across Portuguese being spoken by seasonal workers. Most road, street and place names (and surnames) can be traced to Norman French, although they often receive anglicised pronunciation; some street names are bilingual, with the traditional French version appearing alongside the contemporary English name (not a translation).

LGBTQ+ TRAVELLERS

Guernsey only decriminalised homosexuality in 1983, but today the general attitude of islanders towards the LGBTQ+ community is not so different from that in the UK. Same-sex marriage or partnerships have been officially recognised on Guernsey and Alderney since 2017 and on Sark since 2020. Liberate (www.liberate.gg) is a Guernsey charity which aims to include, inform and support the LGBTQ+ communities across the Channel Islands.

M

MAPS

You can pick up a free up-to-date Perry's map of the island, which also includes Herm, Sark and Alderney, at the Guernsey Information Office in St Peter

Port, also at the bus station, at hotels and many other outlets. The Information Office also has free detailed maps of St Peter Port. For more detail you can purchase *Perry's Guide*, a booklet of road maps with every little lane (www. perrys.gg). A useful and widely available walking map of the island (free of charge) includes suggested walks, with details of walking time, terrain, points of interest and refreshment stops. If you are walking your way around the islands you might also consider the Ordnance Survey-style map of the Bailiwick of Guernsey, with Guernsey at 1:15000, and Alderney, Herm and Sark on the reverse at 1:10000.

MEDIA

All English national newspapers and some European ones arrive in the early morning on the day of publication, weather permitting. *The Guernsey Press* is the island's daily newspaper. The annual *Essential Guernsey Guide*, covering island attractions, eating out and shopping, can be picked up free of charge from the tourist information centre and other outlets. UK national radio and television stations are broadcast in Guernsey and there is a local ITV contractor – Channel Television. There are two local radio stations: BBC Radio Guernsey and the commercial station Island FM.

MONEY

English sterling is freely accepted on the islands, as are all major debit and credit cards. Guernsey also has its own currency, in the same denominations as UK notes and coins, apart from the fact that it still has £1 notes. UK and Guernsey currency can be used within the islands but Channel Island sterling may not be accepted in the UK apart from in banks, which will exchange notes. Some shops will accept euros, normally only in note form, and change will generally be given in sterling. All major debit and credit cards are widely accepted throughout the islands. ATM machines can be found at all of the high street banks in St Peter Port, the airport, some supermarkets, garages and out-of-town banks throughout the island. Sark has no ATMs.

The absence of VAT on the islands and the low duty on imported luxury items is mainly offset by the higher transport costs.

O

OPENING HOURS

Banks. Banks have similar opening hours to those in the UK, with some open on Saturday morning.

Shops. Normal opening times are Mon–Sat 9am–5.30pm. There is no general Sunday opening in Guernsey but some shops in St Peter Port and a few convenience food stores and small supermarkets remain open, especially when a cruise ship arrives.

Tourist attractions. Most museums and tourist attractions are open from April to October from 10am to 5pm, though the times are subject to change and some of the major sites are open all year. For a list of current openings go to the Visit Guernsey website (www.visitguernsey.com).

Pubs. Guernsey licensing hours are Mon–Sat 10am–12.45am, Sun noon–12.45am.

P

POLICE

In an emergency dial 999, for non-emergency calls dial 01481-222 222. The police headquarters are located at Hospital Lane, St Peter Port, GY1 2QN (see also Crime and Safety on page 120).

POST OFFICES

Guernsey runs its own post office and issues its own stamps. Mail leaving Guernsey, Sark or Herm must bear Guernsey postage; from Alderney, both Alderney and Guernsey stamps can be used. Unlike in the UK, mail is not divided into first and second class and note that Guernsey's pillar boxes are normally blue, rather than red. The post office in Market Street, St Peter Port, is open Monday to Friday 8.30am–5pm, Saturday 9am–noon. Channel Island stamps are much in demand by collectors worldwide and the main post office has a philatelic display and stamp sales.

PUBLIC HOLIDAYS

Guernsey has the same public holidays as the UK with an additional day's holiday on 9 May, Liberation Day, commemorating the end of the German Occupation in 1945.

1 January New Year's Day
March or April Good Friday and Easter Monday
First and last Monday in May Spring Bank Holidays
9 May Liberation Day
Last Monday in August August Bank Holiday
25 December Christmas Day
26 December Boxing Day

T

TELEPHONES

The code for Guernsey, Herm, Sark and Alderney is 01481 from the UK and +44 1481 internationally. STD codes for the UK from Guernsey are the same as those used from the UK. Although the code appears to be a UK one, the Channel Islands are excluded from the UK national price rates and the costs of calls are similar to those for Europe. Mobile networks, provided by JT, Sure and Airtel Vodafone, require a roaming facility plus international dialling codes. 'Pay as you go' phones only operate in Guernsey where there is an agreement with the network provider. Check with your provider if in doubt. Coin-operated payphones are located around the island.

TIME ZONES

As in the rest of the UK, the Channel Islands are on Greenwich Mean Time (GMT), with clocks moving forward in late March, and reverting back in late October.

New York	**Guernsey**	Paris	Jo'burg	Sydney	Auckland
7am	**noon**	1pm	2pm	11pm	1am

TIPPING

Hotels and restaurants often add a service charge (10–15 percent) to the bill, in which case there is no need to tip. If service has not been satisfactory, this charge may be deducted from the bill. If the charge has not been added to the bill, 10 percent is an average tip for satisfactory service.

Taxi drivers and hairdressers do not include service charges; a tip of 10 percent is normal for satisfactory service.

TOILETS

There are clean public toilets at main sites and at most beaches. Cafés are usually laid back about the public using their facilities, although if you buy a drink it will be appreciated.

TOURIST INFORMATION

The Guernsey Information Centre (North Esplanade, St Peter Port, tel: 01481-723 552; www.visitguernsey.com; open Mon–Sat 10am–5pm, Sun 10am–1pm, reduced hours in winter) has a wealth of information on the island, including guided walks, exhibitions, theatre bookings and accommodation details. Various free booklets are available on *what to see and do in Guernsey, Herm, Sark and Alderney* and *cycle tours and walks in Guernsey.*

Sark has an information centre on The Avenue (tel: 01481-832 345; www.sark.co.uk). Alderney has a Visitor Information Centre with some excellent walking guides at 51 Victoria Street, St Anne (tel: 01481-822 333; www.visitalderney.com).

TRANSPORT

Guernsey has a variety of transport options, both public and private. The smaller islands, however, leave you with little choice between a bicycle and your own two feet.

Buses. Guernsey's bus service is operated by CT Plus on behalf of the Environment Department. The network services most parts of the island including the main beaches and visitor attractions. Information including routes, fares and timetables can be accessed on www.buses.gg; alternatively information is available from the bus terminal or Visitor Information Centre. A single fare of £1 applies to all journeys (£3 for late-night services after 10pm; contactless payment only). Travel passes are available for one, two and seven days for individuals and families (up to three children under 17 travelling together).

Since many bus stops are served by several routes you are advised to wave down the relevant bus as it approaches. You can also hail a bus and the driver will stop to pick you up provided it is safe to do so (but not in St Peter Port, Bridge or the St Sampson area).

Several companies operate scheduled or tailor-made bus tours, including Island Coachways (tel: 01481-720 210; www.icw.gg) and Intransit (tel: 07781-108 068; www.intransit.gg).

Taxis. Guernsey has licensed taxis at three ranks: in central St Peter Port and St Sampson (on the bridge), and at the airport. Pre-booking is advisable whenever possible. Taxi companies include: A+S Taxis (tel: 07781-125 544), Island Taxis (tel: 01481-700 500) and Donkey Taxis (tel: 07839-747 667).

Carriages (Sark). Horse-drawn carriages on Sark seat six or ten people and normally do one-hour tours in the north of Sark or two-hour tours of the north and south. All tours start and finish at La Collinette, the crossroads at the top of the Harbour Hill.

Inter-island Ferries and France

Herm: Travel Trident (tel: 01481-721 379; www.traveltrident.com) operates ferries from St Peter Port to Herm roughly every hour July to August, with fewer boats during off-peak times. Go early to avoid the day-trippers in the summer. The journey time is 20 minutes.

Sark: The Isle of Sark Shipping Company (tel: 01481-724 059; www.sarkshipping.gg) runs day trips to Sark with generally four ferries most days in summer. The journey time is around 50 minutes.

Alderney: the fastest though not the cheapest way to visit the island of Alderney from Guernsey is to take the 20-minute flight operated by Aurigny (see page 123). Ferry passenger services from Guernsey to Alderney are seasonal but the most extensive scheduled timetable is offered by The Salty Blond (tel: 01481-822 234), which runs from April through to December.

Day trips to Jersey and France: Condor Ferries (www.condorferries.com)

operate day trips from St Peter Port to Jersey and to St Malo in France. Manche Îles Express (tel: 01481-701 316; www.manche-iles.com; currently suspended due to Covid-19 restrictions) operate passenger ferries connecting Guernsey with Jersey, and Carteret, Diélette and Granville in Normandy.

TRAVELLERS WITH DISABILITIES

With all its steps and steep streets, especially in St Peter Port, Guernsey is not ideal for travellers with disabilities. For information on accessibility on the island go to www.accessable.co.uk, which can be used in conjunction with the Visit Guernsey website (www.visitguernsey.com).

On-street parking and public car parks have designated areas for UK and EU blue parking card holders. Guernsey has 'low-floor' buses that are designed to carry disabled passengers. For more information go to www.buses.gg. For wheelchair-accessible taxis contact the Guernsey Information Centre or go to www.visitguernsey.com.

For equipment hire contact the Health Care Equipment Centre (tel: 01481-729 268).

The Radar National Key Scheme, which enables disabled people to access locked public toilets, operates in Guernsey. Visitors are advised to bring their own key; alternatively they are available from the Guernsey Information Centre.

For four-wheel mobility scooters on carless Sark, contact Sark Tourism (tel: 01481-832 345; email: office@sark.co.uk).

V

VISAS AND ENTRY REQUIREMENTS

Guernsey has the same passport and visa requirements as the UK. Although a passport is therefore not necessary for visitors arriving from the UK, airline passengers will need valid photographic ID in order to travel, and a passport is required if you visit France.

As Guernsey is not a full member of the EU, you can still purchase duty-free goods when travelling to and from the island. Maximum allowances are 200 cigarettes or 100 cigarillos or 50 cigars or 250 grams of tobacco; 4 litres of still table wine and 1 litre of spirits or strong liqueurs over 22 per-cent volume or two litres of fortified wine, sparkling wine or other liqueurs; 16 litres of beer or cider; £390-worth of other goods (watches, jewellery, perfume, cameras, etc).

At the time of writing, there are no travel restrictions regarding Covid-19. However, travellers are strongly advised to test before their journey. Travel reg-ulations relating to Covid-19 are subject to change at short notice, so always check the latest advice before you fly.

W

WEBSITES AND INTERNET ACCESS

Many hotels offer Wi-fi, sometimes chargeable. Free Wi-fi hotspots include Guernsey Airport, Guernsey Harbour, Guernsey Visitor Centre, the Guille-Allès Library and a few cafés and pubs.

For the official Guernsey, Sark, Alderney or Herm website visit www.visit-guernsey.com, www.sark.co.uk, www.visitalderney.com and www.herm.com respectively.

The largest community website serving the Channel Islands (www.islan-dlife.org) is full of information about the islands, although not always up to date.

The online version of *The Guernsey Press* (www.guernseypress.com) is great for daily news, information on what's on, tide times and more. Whilst www.guernseytickets.gg is the best source for event ticket sales.

If you are looking for information about museums and galleries on the islands, check out www.museums.gov.gg, which includes event listings and up-to-date information about exhibitions and historic sites. There's also lots of information about things to see and do with children.

For everything you need to know regarding the Guernsey bus service head to www.buses.gg.

If you are looking for information about the current Covid-19 travel regula-tions check www.covid19.gov.gg/guidance/travel/current.

WHERE TO STAY

The choice of accommodation ranges from luxury boutique hotels to simple B&Bs. Self-catering is now very popular, with a choice of over 60 cottages, bungalows or apartments on offer, well suited to those who want to enjoy the island at their own pace, and in their own space. Some offer shared leisure amenities (sometimes with an adjoining hotel), such as swimming pool children's play area and activity options.

The Guernsey Tourism website (www.visitguernsey.com) has a comprehensive section on accommodation. For hotels and self-catering on Herm, Sark and Alderney, visit www.herm.com, www.sark.co.uk and www.visitalderney.com respectively.

Most places will require deposit or credit card details before confirming a reservation, and for special deals you may need to pay in full prior to arrival. VAT is not chargeable in the Channel Islands. Prices fluctuate according to the season, with some great deals in winter. Prices are generally at least as high, if not higher, than the UK, but substantial savings can be made by booking accommodation and travel together as part of a package (see page 116).

Reservations for a holiday in July and August need to be made well in advance. The shoulder months of March, April, May, September and October are, weather permitting, good times of year to travel to Guernsey as rates are lower and accommodation is easier to find. In hotels with restaurants half-board terms are normally available.

Accommodation is rated from one to five stars. Gold and silver accolades are awarded to hotels and self-catering units that consistently deliver service and hospitality above what is required by the star rating.

We have used the following symbols to give an idea of the price of a standard double room and breakfast for two people in high season.

££££	**over £250**
£££	**£180–250**
££	**£130–180**
£	**under £130**

ST PETER PORT

Best Western Hotel de Havelet £££ *Havelet, St Peter Port, tel: 01481-722 199,* www.dehaveletguernsey.com. A Georgian house, 15 minutes' walk uphill from St Peter Port (or courtesy minibus in summer) with fine views of the harbour and islands. Indoor pool with sauna, steam room and jacuzzi.

La Collinette ££ *St Jacques, St Peter Port, tel: 01481-710 331,* www.lacollinette. com. This welcoming family-run hotel with cottages and apartments has a big, sheltered garden and pool. It is a 10-minute walk downhill to St Peter Port, through the Candie Gardens. Contemporary restaurant and bar.

Duke of Normandie ££ *Lefebvre St, St Peter Port, tel: 01481 721431,* www. dukeofnormandie.com. Modern boutique hotel, centrally located in the heart of St Peter Port, with friendy and attentive staff. Boasting 40 newly renovated rooms with en suite bathrooms. Be sure to check out the gastro pub on-site with comfy outdoor seating.

Duke of Richmond Hotel £££ *Cambridge Park, St Peter Port, tel: 01481-726 221,* www.dukeofrichmond.com. This popular four-star hotel beside the Candie Gardens has a contemporary look with its black and white lounge and bar/restaurant leopardskin fabrics. Guest room and suite prices vary substantially depending on views (many overlook the sea) and the degree of luxury – there's also two split-level apartments.

Fermain Valley £££ *St Peter Port, tel: 01481-235 666,* www.fermainvalley. com. Used for business as well as pleasure, this four-star hotel has stunning sea views and is only a 5-minute drive from St Peter Port (traffic permitting). There are five categories of stylish rooms, spread over two separate buildings. A walk down the valley brings you to one of the prettiest bays in Guernsey.

La Frégate Hotel £££ *Les Cotils, St Peter Port, tel: 01481-724 624,* www.lafregatehotel.com. Stylish, boutique hotel in its own grounds in St Peter Port, blending the charm of an 18th-century manor house with the amenities of a modern hotel. Fantastic views across the islands and arguably the best restaurant in Guernsey (see page 106).

The Old Government House Hotel and Spa ££££ *St Ann's Place, St Peter Port, tel: 01481-724 921, www.theoghhotel.com.* The former official residence of Guernsey's governor, the OGH (as it's familiarly known) dates from 1858 and retains many original features. This is the only five-star hotel on the island. Expect plush individually designed bedrooms, top-notch cuisine in the Brasserie or Curry Room, traditional afternoon teas and excellent service. Leisure facilities include a well-equipped spa, gym and outdoor heated pool.

St Pierre Park, Spa and Golf Resort ££ *St Peter Port, tel: 01481-728 282, www.handpickedhotels.co.uk/stpierrepark.* Luxurious but slightly impersonal modern hotel set in 35 acres of parkland on the outskirts of St Peter Port. Ideal for sports enthusiasts with a 9-hole golf course, tennis courts, indoor pool, health club and spa. The various eating options include the Terrace Café Bar & Balcony (see page 107).

Les Rocquettes Hotel £££ *Les Gravees, St Peter Port, tel: 01481-722 146, www.lesrocquettesguernsey.com.* Within walking distance of the town centre of St Peter Port, this former manor house features a total of fifty updated rooms with en suite bathrooms. Amenities include an indoor swimming pool, integrated children's pool, jacuzzi, sauna, steam room and gym. The hotel also offers two self-catering apartments with full access to the hotel's Mulberry Health Suite.

Ziggurat £££ *No. 5 Constitution Steps, tel: 01481-723-008, www.hotelziggurat.com.* Moroccan Riad-inspired décor sets this boutique hotel apart from the rest. Featuring cosy rooms, some with balconies overlooking the harbour, situated in a great location. Make sure to sample dinner on the terrace or in the beautifully decorated restaurant. Tucked away, this hidden gem is only accessible by the Constitution Steps. Be prepared for the climb.

AROUND THE ISLAND

St Martin

La Barbarie ££ *Saints Bay Road, St Martin, tel: 01481-235 217, www.labarbariehotel.com.* The combination of friendly and attentive staff, good food and comfortable, well-equipped guest rooms make this one of Guernsey's most appealing three-star hotels. It's worth paying a bit extra for the 'superior' category rooms which have the space and facilities of a four-star hotel. The location, tucked away in the narrow lanes of St Martin, provides easy access to the cliffs and coves of the south coast.

Bella Luce Hotel ££ *La Fosse, St Martin, tel: 01481-238 764*, www.bellalucehotel.com. This ancient manor house has been transformed into a luxury boutique hotel, one of the most desirable on the island. Down a leafy lane amid lush gardens, it offers opulent guest rooms, some with four-poster beds, a candlelit-restaurant with top quality cuisine, a cellar bar where gin is distilled and a spa.

Hotel La Michele £ *Les Hubits de Bas, St Martin, tel: 01481-238 065*, www.lamichelehotel.com. This small family-run hotel, renowned for hospitality, has its own restaurant and a secluded garden with an attractive heated swimming pool.

La Trelade ££ *Forest Road, St Martin, tel: 01481-235 454*, www.latreladehotel.co.uk. Set back from the road in its own gardens the hotel is only half a mile from Guernsey's scenic south coast with its cliff top walks; it's also close to the main bus routes. Good leisure facilities include health suite with indoor pool and gym.

St Saviour

Driftwood Inn £ *Perelle Bay, St Saviour, tel: 01481-264 436*, www.driftwoodinn.co.uk. Overlooking Perelle Bay on the west coast of Guernsey, this popular budget hotel providing an ideal mix of value, comfort and convenience, in a family-friendly setting with an array of amenities. The furnished sun terrace makes a visit even more pleasant. The property also features a pool and an on-site restaurant.

The Farmhouse £££ *Route des Bas Courtils, St Saviour, tel: 01481-264 181*, www.thefarmhouse.gg. Run by the Nussbaumer family for three generations, this four-star boutique hotel is one of Guernsey's favourite places to stay. The 14 bedrooms are furnished in contemporary style, with large walk-in showers. Dependent on the season, the popular restaurant offers meals available by the fire, poolside or in one of the gazebos.

Castel

Cobo Bay Hotel ££ *Coast Road, Cobo, Castel, tel: 01481-257 102,* www.cobobayhotel.com. Ideal beach holiday hotel with good-value rooms across the road from Cobo Bay. The award-winning restaurant, renowned for seafood, has a spacious terrace with unparalleled sea and sunset views. Small complimentary health suite.

Fauxquets Valley Campsite £ *Candie Road, Castel, tel: 01481-255 460,* www.fauxquets.co.uk. Wonderful campsite in a tranquil valley. Excellent amenities include heated pool, restaurant and bar, shop and children's playground and games room.

Fleur du Jardin ££ *Kings Mills, Castel, tel: 01481-257 996,* www.fleurdujardin.com. Named after a breed of Guernsey cow, this old farmhouse has been stylishly renovated and offers 14 individually designed en suite rooms with bleached timber walls and sandstone wet rooms. Some rooms offer sea views or direct access to the private garden. Features a first-class gastro-pub, a solar-heated pool and a health suite.

Le Frequet ££ *Rue du Frequet, Castel, tel: 01481-256 509,* www.lefriquethotel.com. A sweeping drive allows first glimpse of the hotel across extensive landscaped grounds. Relax in a comfortable lounge, take a drink in Eddie's Bar, or dine in the Lobster and Grill, which serves some of the best Guernsey seafood. Other facilities include an outdoor heated swimming pool and a pretty patio fronting the gardens. The 37 guest rooms are spacious, and there is a two-bed, villa style lodge set in the gardens.

Wayside Cheer £ *Grandes Rocques, Castel, tel: 01481-257 290,* www.waysidecheerhotel.com. This very friendly hotel, overlooking the beautiful sandy Grandes Rocques Bay, is great value for money and ideal for families. Outside there is a heated outdoor swimming pool surrounded by lovely gardens and a terrace perfect for alfresco drinking and eating. Other amenities include a restaurant, bar, games room, TV lounge and free Wi-fi; and live entertainment is provided at the weekends. All rooms are en suite and the family rooms can accommodate up to five.

Torteval

Clifftop Cottages *Le Petit Manoir, Route de Pleinmont, tel: 01481-263 090,* www.clifftopcottages.com. Three self-catering cottages sleeping between 2 and 7 in a peaceful, rural part of the island close to stunning cliff walks. Private patio areas with garden furniture. Available year-round; £400-£800 per week depending on size and season.

The Imperial ££ *Rocquaine Bay, tel: 01481-264 044,* www.theimperial.gg. Perfectly located opposite the beach, this hotel features 16 recently redecorated en suite bedrooms, some of which have stunning views of the bay. This is a great place to use as your base while you enjoy the south coast cliff paths. There's also a restaurant with alfresco dining on-site.

Vale

The Bay Apartments *Vale, tel: 07781-145 129,* www.thebayguernsey.co.uk. Six spacious, self-catering apartments, some with spectacular views of sandy Pembroke Bay. Facilities include tennis, outdoor swimming pool and health and beauty salon. Convenient for golfers with L'Ancresse Golf Club nearby. £550–£1,700 per week depending on size and season.

Peninsula Hotel ££ *Les Dicqs, Vale, tel: 01481-248 400,* www.peninsula.gg. This 99-room hotel overlooks Grand Havre Bay and its extensive, landscaped gardens have direct access to the beach. Atmosphere is a bit impersonal, but facilities are plentiful, particularly for families, with outdoor and children's pool.

Herm

White House Hotel £££ *Herm, tel: 01481-750 000,* www.herm.com; *closed off-season.* In a harbour-side setting, this is an ideal place to unwind away from the 21st century (no TVs here). It has been family-run for over half a century and the emphasis is on old-fashioned values, good service and culinary excellence. Amenities include a solar-heated swimming pool, a tennis court, a croquet lawn – or books and board games when the weather is inclement. Cottages are also available.

Sark

La Moinerie Hotel ££ *Sark, tel: 01481-832 089*, www.lamoineriehotel.com. Secreted away on the west side of Sark, this charming hotel is reached by a cobbled lane, and stands on the site of a medieval monastery. Lovingly restored, its rustic simplicity and charm are complemented by the highest standards of guest rooms, which are housed in the main stone farmhouse and in nine luxury lodges (that can sleep four adults) scattered about the grounds.

La Sablonnerie £££ *Little Sark, tel: 01481-832 061, www.sablonneriesark. com; closed off-season.* Located on Little Sark, this remote farmhouse hotel is reached by the owner's horse-drawn carriages and offers rural tranquillity with secluded cottage garden and croquet lawn. Most guests dine here and make the most of the excellent cuisine (see page 113). Features cosy lounge with log fire. One of the loveliest hotels on the Channel Islands providing a total escape.

Stocks Hotel ££££ *Sark, tel: 01481-832 001*, www.stockshotel.com. A family-owned country house in the wooded valley leading to Dixcart Bay. The Dame of Sark used to entertain royalty here and an escape tunnel survives from the days of the German Occupation when officers, including the Commandant, were billeted here. Features 23 comfortable en suite guest rooms with free Wi-fi. Rooms range from luxury suites to family combinations and pet friendly rooms with everything you need to keep your furry friend comfortable during your stay. Menus feature home-made and local produce (see page 113).

Sue's B&B £ *Cae de Met, Sark, tel: 01481-832 107; closed Jan–Easter*, www. suebnb.com. Sue Guille owns and runs this wonderful B&B with three garden-and-sea-view en suite guest rooms, and one smaller room. Breakfast is taken on the sunny veranda or in the beautiful garden. Sue's husband George operates boat trips around the island.

Alderney

Braye Beach Hotel £££, *Braye Street, Alderney, tel: 0800-280 0550 (UK free-phone)*, www.brayebeach.com. Chic designer hotel with a perfect setting overlooking Braye Beach. There are four categories of bedrooms – all are light and bright and have free Wi-fi. Book ahead for sea-view rooms as they are popular and fill up quick. Other facilities include a 19-seat cinema, three options for eating and drinking (a beach bar, brasserie and a wine vault turned steakhouse restaurant and cocktail bar) and a terrace overlooking Braye beach.

Farm Court £ *Le Petit Val, Alderney, tel: 01481-822 075*, www.farmcourt-alderney.co.uk. This good-value B&B, in a collection of small, converted barns set around an enclosed cobbled courtyard, is run by a friendly husband-and-wife team who prepare generous breakfasts made from locally produced ingredients. All 12 comfortable rooms feature en suite bathrooms with access to the guest lounge and courtyard. A self-catering cottage that sleeps three is also available.

Fort Clonque *Alderney (book through the Landmark Trust, tel: 01628-825 925*, www.landmarktrust.org.uk. Built in the 1840s, Fort Clonque has been converted by the Landmark Trust into self-catering accommodation, with sleeping quarters for up to 13 people (or 14 if you count the ghost!), in four different buildings. Being cut off from Alderney at high tide, it suits those with a sense of adventure. Four nights from £879.

Georgian House £ *Alderney, tel: 01481-822 471*, www.georgianalderney.com. Centrally located hotel featuring four comfortable rooms with en suite bathrooms. The restaurant on-site is well worth a visit, with fresh and local ingredients at its heart. They also do a fantastic breakfast for hotel guests. Make sure you visit the wonderful, secluded gardens; the perfect place to while away the afternoon.

INDEX

THE **MINI** ROUGH GUIDE TO
GUERNSEY

First Edition 2022

Editor: Beth Williams
Author: Jackie Staddon
Picture Editor: Tom Smyth
Cartography Update: Carte
Layout: Pradeep Thapliyal
Head of DTP and Pre-Press: Katie Bennett
Head of Publishing: Kate Drynan
Photography Credits: Alamy 4TR; Anna
Mockford & Nick Bonetti/Apa Publications 4MC,
4MC, 4ML, 4ML, 5M, 6T, 6B, 7T, 7B, 11, 13, 15, 16,
19, 21, 24, 27, 29, 30, 33, 34, 36, 38, 41, 42, 43,
44, 45, 47, 49, 51, 52, 55, 56, 57, 58, 62, 63, 65,
66, 68, 69, 71, 73, 75, 78, 80, 82, 84, 86, 89, 90,
92, 93, 95, 96, 98, 99, 101, 104; iStock 4TL, 5M;
Shutterstock 5T; Visit Guernsey/Chris George
Photography 1, 4TC
Cover Credits: St Peter Port **Shutterstock**

Distribution
UK, Ireland and Europe: Apa Publications (UK)
Ltd; sales@roughguides.com
United States and Canada: Ingram Publisher
Services; ips@ingramcontent.com
Australia and New Zealand: Booktopia;
retailer@booktopia.com.au
Worldwide: Apa Publications (UK) Ltd;
sales@roughguides.com

**Special Sales, Content Licensing
and CoPublishing**
Rough Guides can be purchased in bulk
quantities at discounted prices. We can create
special editions, personalised jackets and
corporate imprints tailored to your needs. sales@
roughguides.com; http://roughguides.com

Contact us
Every effort has been made to provide accurate
information in this publication, but changes
are inevitable. The publisher cannot be held
responsible for any resulting loss, inconvenience
or injury sustained by any traveller as a result of
information or advice contained in the guide.
We would appreciate it if readers would call our
attention to any errors or outdated information,
or if you feel we've left something out. Please
send your comments with the subject line
"Rough Guide Mini Guernsey Update" to
mail@uk.roughguides.com.